HEINEMANN PLAYS

TENNESSEE WILLIAMS

A STREETCAR NAMED DESIRE

**Introduction and questions by
Ray Speakman**

Heinemann

Heinemann Educational,
a division of Heinemann Publishers (Oxford) Ltd
Halley Court, Jordan Hill, Oxford OX2 8EJ
OXFORD LONDON EDINBURGH
MADRID ATHENS BOLOGNA PARIS
MELBOURNE SYDNEY AUCKLAND SINGAPORE TOKYO
IBADAN NAIROBI HARARE GABORONE PORTSMOUTH NH (USA)

First published by Methuen in 1984 by arrangement with Secker and Warburg Ltd.
First published in Hereford Plays by Heinemann/Methuen 1989
First published in Heinemann Plays 1995

10 9 8 7 6 5 4 3 2
99 98 97 96 95

ISBN 0 435 23310 6

Original design by Jeffery White Creative Associates; adapted by Jim Turner

Typeset by TechType, Abingdon, Oxon

Printed in England by Clays Ltd, St Ives plc

CONTENTS

PREFACE

In this edition of *A Streetcar Named Desire*, you will find notes, questions and activities to help in studying the play in class, particularly at GCSE level and above.

The introduction provides background information on the author and his other works, and the circumstances and impact of its first production.

The activities at the end of the book range from straight-forward *Keeping Track* questions which can be tackled at the end of each act to focus close attention on what is happening in the play, through more detailed work on characters and themes in *Explorations*.

If you are already using the Hereford edition of *A Streetcar Named Desire*, you will find that the page numbering in the actual playscript is the same, allowing the two editions to be easily used side by side.

INTRODUCTION

Tennessee Williams and A Streetcar Named Desire

Thomas Lanier Williams was born in Columbus, Mississippi on March 26th, 1911. He assumed the name "Tennessee" in 1938 because, he said, "The Williamses fought the Indians for Tennessee, and I had already discovered that the life of a young writer was going to be something similar to the defence of the stockade against a band of savages" – a description reminiscent of Blanche's battles with Stanley in *A Streetcar Named Desire*. Indeed, it has been repeatedly pointed out by critics, biographers and Williams himself, that his plays were very much an exploration and a working out of his own life.

His father, Cornelius Coffin Williams, a hard drinking, bad tempered, coarse man who called his son "Miss Nancy", was often absent from the household – he had "fallen in love with long distances" like the father in *The Glass Menagerie* – in his work for the telephone company, and later, for a shoe company. Tennessee's mother was Edwina Dakin, the daughter of an Episcopal minister. She despised her husband's drinking and womanising; she felt she had an aristocratic pedigree which was ill-suited to the life her husband, and his frequent changes of address, forced her to lead. "CC" Williams and Edwina Dakin had three children: Rose, born in 1907, Tom, born in 1911 and Dakin, born in 1919 – shortly after the family's traumatic move to St Louis. In St Louis the family were separated from Edwina's genteel background – she was thirty-four and had to cook for the first time – an experience which Tom later described as losing "belief in everything but loss". As a result, Tom withdrew into his writing, Edwina into dreams of lost Southern gentility, and Tom's sister, Rose, into madness – she was lobotomized in 1937. Edwina Dakin Williams, similarly, ended her life in a mental home.

Tennessee Williams's first major success was *The Glass Menagerie* (1944), his second was *A Streetcar Named Desire* (1947). In an article in the *New York Times* (30.11.47) Williams describes the disadvantages of sudden fame – "the catastrophe of success," which he had experienced following his first successful play. He felt that the material security he found following *The Glass Menagerie* had limited his creativity. He felt that *Streetcar* rediscovered this creativity – and in many ways this battle between humanity and the corrupting effect of security is an important theme in the play.

When *Streetcar* was first performed in England in 1949 it attracted a good deal of the "wrong" sort of attention: it was serialised in one of the more excitable Sunday newspapers and was popularly thought to be sexually permissive in the extreme. The play's early reputation, however, was short lived; critics and audiences quickly came to see Williams's play for what it really is – a work of great humanity and technical brilliance. Indeed, it is not too grand a claim to suggest that *A Streetcar Named Desire* is a classic tragedy. The poet Keats identified a tragic hero as an individual unable to see that life has its impossibilities. Tennessee Williams's contemporary, Arthur Miller, maintained that the struggle of a tragic hero, "is that of the individual attempting to gain his rightful place in society … ready to lay down his life, if need be, to secure one thing – his sense of personal dignity." Keats and Miller would, I think, have recognised in Blanche the individual they had in mind – unable to renounce the image of herself as a rare being, unable to accept, as her sister does, the "blisses of the commonplace".

Between his success with *Streetcar* and 1962 Tennessee Williams produced a large number of highly acclaimed plays: *Summer and Smoke* (1948), *The Rose Tattoo* (1951), *Camino*

Real (1953), *Cat on a Hot Tin Roof* (1955), *Orpheus Descending* (1957), *Suddenly Last Summer* (1958), *Sweet Bird of Youth* (1959), *Period of Adjustment* (1960), *Night of the Iguana* (1961) and *The Milk Train Doesn't Stop Here Anymore* (1962). *Night of the Iguana* is considered by many to be his last great play, and although his reputation declined in subsequent years, he continued writing until his death (by accidentally choking on a bottle top) in 1983.

In 1976 Williams published his *Memoirs*. He wrote to his agent shortly before their publication: "I have a new title for my memoirs – 'Flee, Flee This Sad Hotel' – it's a quote from a poem by Anne Sexton. Of course hotel is a metaphor for my life – and flight from it – if not an impulse – at least is an imminence." He never used the title.

Following the text of the play you will find a series of **Activities and Explorations**. Although these are by no means exhaustive, they are, inevitably, fairly detailed. Their purpose is to encourage a close reading of the text and to stimulate thought, discussion and writing. Many of the suggestions for assignments are shaped with GCSE coursework and A level critical essays in mind.

Whatever your purpose in reading the play, you will find *A Streetcar Named Desire* eminently approachable, and a richly rewarding play to study in depth.

Ray Speakman

A STREETCAR NAMED DESIRE

And so it was I entered the broken world
To trace the visionary company of love, its voice
An instant in the wind (I know not whither hurled)
But not for long to hold each desperate choice.

"THE BROKEN TOWER" BY HART CRANE

Characters

BLANCHE	A NEGRO WOMAN
STELLA	A DOCTOR
STANLEY	A NURSE
MITCH	A YOUNG COLLECTOR
EUNICE	A MEXICAN WOMAN
STEVE	A TAMALE VENDOR
PABLO	

The first London production of this play was at the Aldwych Theatre on Wednesday, October 12th 1949, with the following cast:

BLANCHE DUBOIS	Vivien Leigh
STELLA KOWALSKI	Renee Asherson
STANLEY KOWALSKI	Bonar Colleano
HAROLD MITCHELL (MITCH)	Bernard Braden
EUNICE HUBBEL	Eileen Dale
STEVE HUBBEL	Lyn Evans
PABLO GONZALES	Theodore Bikel
NEGRO WOMAN	Bruce Howard
A STRANGE MAN (DOCTOR)	Sidney Monckton
A STRANGE WOMAN (NURSE)	Mona Lilian
A YOUNG COLLECTOR	John Forrest
A MEXICAN WOMAN	Eileen Way

Directed by LAURENCE OLIVIER
Setting and lighting by JO MIELZINER
Costumes by BEATRICE DAWSON

A STREETCAR NAMED DESIRE

SCENE ONE

The exterior of a two-storey corner building on a street in New Orleans which is named Elysian Fields and runs between the L & N tracks and the river. The section is poor but, unlike corresponding sections in other American cities, it has a raffish charm. The houses are mostly white frame, weathered grey, with rickety outside stairs and galleries and quaintly ornamented gables to the entrances of both. It is first dark of an evening early in May. The sky that shows around the dim white building is a peculiarly tender blue, almost turquoise, which invests the scene with a kind of lyricism and gracefully attenuates the atmosphere of decay. You can almost feel the warm breath of the brown river beyond the river warehouses with their faint redolences of bananas and coffee. A corresponding air is evoked by the music of Negro entertainers at a bar-room around the corner. In this part of New Orleans you are practically always just around the corner, or a few doors down the street, from a tinny piano being played with the infatuated fluency of brown fingers. This "Blue Piano" expresses the spirit of the life which goes on here.

Two women, one white and one coloured, are taking the air on the steps of the building. The white woman is EUNICE, *who occupies the upstairs flat; the coloured woman a neighbour, for New Orleans is a cosmopolitan city where there is a relatively warm and easy intermingling of races in the old part of town. Above the music of the "Blue Piano" the voices of people on the street can be heard overlapping.*

NEGRO WOMAN   (*to* EUNICE) … she says St. Barnabas would send out his dog to lick her and when he did she'd feel an icy cold wave all up an' down her. Well, that night when –

A MAN   (*to a* SAILOR) You keep right on going and you'll find it. You'll hear them tapping on the shutters.

SAILOR   (*to* NEGRO WOMAN *and* EUNICE) Where's the Four Deuces?

VENDOR   Red hot! Red hots!

NEGRO WOMAN   Don't waste your money in that clip joint!

SAILOR   I've got a date there.

VENDOR   Re-e-ed h-o-o-t!

NEGRO WOMAN   Don't let them sell you a Blue Moon cocktail or you won't go out on your own feet!

Two men come around the corner, STANLEY KOWALSKI *and* MITCH. *They are about twenty-eight or thirty years old, roughly dressed in blue denim work clothes.* STANLEY *carries his bowling jacket and a red-stained package from a butcher's.*

STANLEY   (*to* MITCH) Well, what did he say?

MITCH   He said he'd give us even money.

STANLEY   Naw! We gotta have odds!

They stop at the foot of the steps.

STANLEY   (*bellowing*) Hey, there! Stella, Baby!

STELLA *comes out on the first-floor landing, a gentle young woman, about twenty-five, and of a background obviously quite different from her husband's.*

STELLA   (*mildly*) Don't holler at me like that. Hi, Mitch.

STANLEY   Catch!

STELLA   What?

STANLEY Meat!

He heaves the package at her. She cries out in protest but manages to catch it; then she laughs breathlessly. Her husband and his companion have already started back around the corner.

STELLA (*calling after him*) Stanley! Where are you going?

STANLEY Bowling!

STELLA Can I come watch?

STANLEY Come on. (*He goes out.*)

STELLA Be over soon. (*To the white woman*). Hello, Eunice. How are you?

EUNICE I'm all right. Tell Steve to get him a poor boy's sandwich 'cause nothing's left here.

They all laugh; the COLOURED WOMAN *does not stop.* STELLA *goes out.*

NEGRO WOMAN What was that package he th'ew at 'er?

She rises from steps, laughing louder.

EUNICE You hush, now!

NEGRO WOMAN Catch *what*!

She continues to laugh. BLANCHE *comes around the corner, carrying a valise. She looks at a slip of paper, then at the building, then again at the slip and again at the building. Her expression is one of shocked disbelief. Her appearance is incongruous to this setting. She is daintily dressed in a white suit with a fluffy bodice, necklace and earrings of pearl, white gloves and hat, looking as if she were arriving at a summer tea or cocktail party in the garden district. She is above five years older than* STELLA. *Her delicate beauty must avoid a strong light. There is something about her uncertain manner, as well as her white clothes, that suggest a moth.*

EUNICE   (*finally*) What's the matter, honey? Are you lost?

BLANCHE   (*with faintly hysterical humour*) They told me to take a streetcar named Desire, and then transfer to one called Cemeteries and ride six blocks and get off at – Elysian Fields!

EUNICE   That's where you are now.

BLANCHE   At Elysian Fields?

EUNICE   This here is Elysian Fields.

BLANCHE   They mustn't have – understood – what number I wanted…

EUNICE   What number you lookin' for?

BLANCHE *wearily refers to the slip of paper.*

BLANCHE   Six thirty-two.

EUNICE   You don't have to look no further.

BLANCHE   (*uncomprehendingly*) I'm looking for my sister, Stella DuBois. I mean – Mrs. Stanley Kowalski.

EUNICE   That's the party. – You just did miss her, though.

BLANCHE   This – can this be – her home?

EUNICE   She's got the downstairs here and I got the up.

BLANCHE   Oh. She's – out?

EUNICE   You noticed that bowling alley around the corner?

BLANCHE   I'm – not sure I did.

EUNICE   Well, that's where she's at, watchin' her husband bowl. (*There is a pause.*) You want to leave your suitcase here an' go find her?

BLANCHE   No.

NEGRO WOMAN   I'll go tell her you come.

BLANCHE   Thanks.

NEGRO WOMAN   You welcome. (*She goes out.*)

EUNICE   She wasn't expecting you?

BLANCHE   No. No, not tonight.

EUNICE   Well, why don't you just go in and make yourself at home till they get back.

BLANCHE   How could I – do that?

EUNICE   We own this place so I can let you in.

She gets up and opens the downstairs door. A light goes on behind the blind, turning it light blue. BLANCHE *slowly follows her into the downstairs flat. The surrounding areas dim out as the interior is lighted. Two rooms can be seen, not too clearly defined. The one first entered is primarily a kitchen but contains a folding bed to be used by* BLANCHE. *The room beyond this is a bedroom. Off this room is a narrow door to a bathroom.*

EUNICE   (*defensively, noticing* BLANCHE'*s look*) It's sort of messed up right now but when it's clean it's real sweet.

BLANCHE   Is it?

EUNICE   Uh-huh, I think so. So you're Stella's sister?

BLANCHE   Yes. (*Wanting to get rid of her.*) Thanks for letting me in.

EUNICE   *Por nada*, as the Mexicans say, *por nada*! Stella spoke of you.

BLANCHE   Yes?

EUNICE   I think she said you taught school.

BLANCHE   Yes.

EUNICE   And you're from Mississippi, huh?

BLANCHE   Yes.

EUNICE   She showed me a picture of your home-place, the plantation.

BLANCHE   Belle Reve?

EUNICE   A great big place with white columns.

BLANCHE   Yes...

EUNICE   A place like that must be awful hard to keep up.

BLANCHE	If you will excuse me, I'm just about to drop.
EUNICE	Sure, honey. Why don't you set down?
BLANCHE	What I meant was I'd like to be left alone.
EUNICE	(*offended*) Aw. I'll make myself scarce, in that case.
BLANCHE	I didn't mean to be rude, but –
EUNICE	I'll drop by the bowling alley an' hustle her up.

(*She goes out of the door.*)

BLANCHE *sits in a chair very stiffly with her shoulders slightly hunched and her legs pressed close together and her hands tightly clutching her purse as if she were quite cold. After a while the blind look goes out of her eyes and she begins to look slowly around. A cat screeches. She catches her breath with a startled gesture. Suddenly she notices something in a half opened closet. She springs up and crosses to it, and removes a whisky bottle. She pours a half tumbler of whisky and tosses it down. She carefully replaces the bottle and washes out the tumbler at the sink. Then she resumes her seat in front of the table.*

BLANCHE   (*faintly to herself*) I've got to keep hold of myself!

STELLA *comes quickly around the corner of the building and runs to the door of the downstairs flat.*

STELLA   (*calling out joyfully*) Blanche!

For a moment they stare at each other. Then BLANCHE *springs up and runs to her with a wild cry.*

BLANCHE   Stella, oh, Stella, Stella! Stella for Star!

She begins to speak with feverish vivacity as if she feared for either of them to stop and think. They catch each other in a spasmodic embrace.

BLANCHE	Now, then, let me look at you. But don't you look at me, Stella, no, no, no, not till later, not till I've bathed and rested! And turn that over-light off! Turn that off! I won't be looked at in this merciless glare! (STELLA *laughs and complies*.) Come back here now! Oh, my baby! Stella! Stella for Star! (*She embraces her again*.) I thought you would never come back to this horrible place! What am I saying? I didn't mean to say that. I meant to be nice about it and say – Oh, what a convenient location and such – Ha-a-ah! Precious lamb! You haven't said a *word* to me.
STELLA	You haven't given me a chance to, honey! (*She laughs but her glance at* BLANCHE *is a little anxious*.)
BLANCHE	Well, now you talk. Open your pretty mouth and talk while I look around for some liquor! I know you must have some liquor in the place! Where could it be, I wonder? Oh, I spy, I spy!

She rushes to the closet and removes the bottle; she is shaking all over and panting for breath as she tries to laugh. The bottle nearly slips from her grasp.

STELLA	(*noticing*) Blanche, you sit down and let me pour the drinks. I don't know what we've got to mix with. Maybe a coke's in the icebox. Look'n see, honey, while I'm –
BLANCHE	No coke, honey, not with my nerves tonight! Where – where – where is –?
STELLA	Stanley? Bowling! He loves it. They're having a – found some soda! – tournament …
BLANCHE	Just water, baby, to chase it! Now don't get worried, your sister hasn't turned into a drunkard, she's just all shaken up and hot and tired and dirty! You sit down, now, and explain this place to me! What are you

doing in a place like this?

STELLA Now, Blanche –

BLANCHE Oh, I'm sure not going to be a hypocritical, I'm going to be honestly critical about it! Never, never, never in my worst dreams could I picture – Only Poe! Only Mr Edgar Allan Poe! – could do it justice! Out there I suppose is the ghoul-haunted woodland of Weir! (*She laughs.*)

STELLA No, honey, those are the L & N tracks.

BLANCHE No, now seriously, putting joking aside. Why didn't you tell me, why didn't you write me, honey, why didn't you let me know?

STELLA (*carefully, pouring herself a drink*) Tell you what, Blanche?

BLANCHE Why, that you had to live in these conditions?

STELLA Aren't you being a little intense about it? It's not that bad at all! New Orleans isn't like other cities.

BLANCHE This has got nothing to do with New Orleans. You might as well say – forgive me, blessed baby! (*She suddenly stops short.*) The subject is closed!

STELLA (*a little drily*) Thanks.

During the pause, BLANCHE *stares at her. She smiles at* BLANCHE.

BLANCHE (*looking down at her glass, which shakes in her hand*) You're all I've got in the world, and you're not glad to see me!

STELLA (*sincerely*) Why, Blanche, you know that's not true.

BLANCHE No? – I'd forgotten how quiet you were.

STELLA You never did give me a chance to say much, Blanche. So I just got in the habit of being quiet around you.

BLANCHE   (*vaguely*) A good habit to get into… (*Then abruptly.*) You haven't asked me how I happened to get away from the school before the spring term ended.

STELLA   Well, I thought you'd volunteer that information – if you wanted to tell me.

BLANCHE   You thought I'd been fired?

STELLA   No, I – thought you might have – resigned…

BLANCHE   I was so exhausted by all I'd been through my – nerves broke. (*Nervously tamping cigarette.*) I was on the verge of – lunacy, almost! So Mr Graves – Mr Graves is the high school superintendent – he suggested I take a leave of absence. I couldn't put all of those details into the wire… (*She drinks quickly.*) Oh, this buzzes right through me and feels so *good*!

STELLA   Won't you have another?

BLANCHE   No, one's my limit.

STELLA   Sure?

BLANCHE   You haven't said a word about my appearance.

STELLA   You look just fine.

BLANCHE   God love you for a liar! Daylight never exposed so total a ruin! But you – you've put on some weight, yes, you're as plump as a little partridge! And it's so becoming to you!

STELLA   No, Blanche –

BLANCHE   Yes, it is, it is or I wouldn't say it! You just have to watch around the hips a little. Stand up.

STELLA   Not now.

BLANCHE   You hear me? I said stand up! (STELLA *complies reluctantly.*) You messy child, you, you've spilt something on that pretty white lace collar! About your hair – you ought to have it cut in a feather bob with your dainty features. Stella, you have a maid, don't you?

STELLA   No. With only two rooms it's –

BLANCHE	What? *Two* rooms, did you say?
STELLA	This one and – (*She is embarrassed.*)
BLANCHE	The other one? (*She laughs sharply. There is an embarrassed silence.*) How quiet you are, you're so peaceful. Look how you sit there with your little hands folded like a cherub in choir!
STELLA	(*uncomfortably*) I never had anything like your energy, Blanche.
BLANCHE	Well, I never had your beautiful self-control. I am going to take just one little tiny nip more, sort of to put the stopper on, so to speak…Then put the bottle away so I won't be tempted. (*She rises.*) I want you to look at *my* figure! (*She turns around.*) You know I haven't put on one ounce in ten years, Stella? I weigh what I weighed the summer you left Belle Reve. The summer Dad died and you left us…
STELLA	(*a little wearily*) It's just incredible, Blanche, how well you're looking.
BLANCHE	You see I still have that awful vanity about my looks even now that my looks are slipping! (*She laughs nervously and glances at* STELLA *for reassurance.*)
STELLA	(*dutifully*) They haven't slipped one particle.
BLANCHE	After all I've been through? You think I believe that story? Blessed child! (*She touches her forehead shakily.*) Stella, there's – only two rooms?
STELLA	And a bathroom.
BLANCHE	Oh, you do have a bathroom! First door to the right at the top of the stairs? (*They both laugh uncomfortably.*) But, Stella, I don't see where you're going to put me!
STELLA	We're going to put you in here.
BLANCHE	What kind of bed's this – one of those collapsible things? (*She sits on it.*)

STELLA   Does it feel all right?

BLANCHE   (*dubiously*) Wonderful, honey. I don't like a bed that gives much. But there's no door between the two rooms, and Stanley – will it be decent?

STELLA   Stanley is Polish, you know.

BLANCHE   Oh, yes. They're something like Irish, aren't they?

STELLA   Well –

BLANCHE   Only not so – highbrow? (*They both laugh again in the same way.*) I brought some nice clothes to meet all your lovely friends in.

STELLA   I'm afraid you won't think they are lovely.

BLANCHE   What are they like?

STELLA   They're Stanley's friends.

BLANCHE   Polacks?

STELLA   They're a mixed lot, Blanche.

BLANCHE   Heterogeneous-types?

STELLA   Oh, yes. Yes, types is right!

BLANCHE   Well – anyhow – I brought nice clothes and I'll wear them. I guess you're hoping I'll say I'll put up at a hotel, but I'm not going to put up at a hotel. I want to be *near* you, got to be *with* somebody, I *can't be alone*! Because – as you must have noticed – I'm – *not* very *well*... (*Her voice drops and her look is frightened.*)

STELLA   You seem a little nervous or overwrought or something.

BLANCHE   Will Stanley like me, or will I be just a visiting in-law, Stella? I couldn't stand that.

STELLA   You'll get along fine together, if you'll just try not to – well – compare him with men that we went out with at home.

BLANCHE   Is he so – different?

STELLA   Yes. A different species.

BLANCHE　In what way; what's he like?

STELLA　Oh, you can't describe someone you're in love with! Here's a picture of him! (*She hands a photograph to* BLANCHE.)

BLANCHE　An officer?

STELLA　A Master Sergeant in the Engineers' Corps. Those are decorations!

BLANCHE　He had those on when you met him?

STELLA　I assure you I wasn't just blinded by all the brass.

BLANCHE　That's not what I –

STELLA　But of course there were things to adjust myself to later on.

BLANCHE　Such as his civilian background! (STELLA *laughs uncertainly.*) How did he take it when you said I was coming?

STELLA　Oh, Stanley doesn't know yet.

BLANCHE　(*frightened*) You – haven't told him?

STELLA　He's on the road a good deal.

BLANCHE　Oh. Travels?

STELLA　Yes.

BLANCHE　Good. I mean – isn't it?

STELLA　(*half to herself*) I can hardly stand it when he is away for a night…

BLANCHE　Why, Stella?

STELLA　When he's away for a week I nearly go wild!

BLANCHE　Gracious!

STELLA　And when he comes back I cry on his lap like a baby… (*She smiles to herself.*)

BLANCHE　I guess that is what is meant by being in love… (STELLA *looks up with a radiant smile.*) Stella –

STELLA　What?

BLANCHE　(*in an uneasy rush*) I haven't asked you the things you probably thought I was going to ask. And so I'll expect you to be understanding about what *I* have to tell *you*.

STELLA   What, Blanche? (*Her face turns anxious.*)

BLANCHE   Well, Stella – you're going to reproach me, I know that you're bound to reproach me – but before you do – take into consideration – you left! I stayed and struggled! You came to New Orleans and looked out for yourself! *I* stayed at Belle Reve and tried to hold it together! I'm not meaning this in any reproachful way, but *all* the burden descended on *my* shoulders.

STELLA   The best I could do was make my own living, Blanche.

BLANCHE *begins to shake again with intensity.*

BLANCHE   I know, I know. But you are the one that abandoned Belle Reve, not I! I stayed and fought for it, bled for it, almost died for it!

STELLA   Stop this hysterical outburst and tell me what's happened? What do you mean fought and bled? What kind of –

BLANCHE   I knew you would, Stella. I knew you would take this attitude about it!

STELLA   About – what? – please!

BLANCHE   (*slowly*) The loss – the loss…

STELLA   Belle Reve? Lost, is it? No!

BLANCHE   Yes, Stella.

They stare at each other across the yellow-checked linoleum of the table. BLANCHE *slowly nods her head and* STELLA *looks slowly down at her hands folded on the table. The music of the "blue piano" grows louder.* BLANCHE *touches her handkerchief to her forehead.*

STELLA   But how did it go? What happened?

BLANCHE (*springing up*) You're a fine one to ask me how it went!

STELLA Blanche!

BLANCHE You're a fine one to sit there *accusing me* of it!

STELLA *Blanche!*

BLANCHE I, I, *I* took the blows in my face and my body! All of those deaths! The long parade to the graveyard! Father, mother! Margaret, that dreadful way! So big with it, it couldn't be put in a coffin! But had to be burned like rubbish! You just came home in time for the funerals, Stella. And funerals are pretty compared to deaths. Funerals are quiet, but deaths – not always. Sometimes their breathing is hoarse, and sometimes it rattles, and sometimes they even cry out to you, "Don't let me go!" Even the old, sometimes, say, "Don't let me go." As if you were able to stop them! But funerals are quiet, with pretty flowers. And, oh, what gorgeous boxes they pack them away in! Unless you were there at the bed when they cried out, "Hold me!" you'd never suspect there was the struggle for breath and bleeding. You didn't dream, but I saw! *Saw! Saw!* And now you sit there telling me with your eyes that I let the place go! How in hell do you think all that sickness and dying was paid for? Death is expensive, Miss Stella! And old Cousin Jessie's right after Margaret's, hers! Why, the Grim Reaper had put up his tent on our doorstep!...Stella. Belle Reve was his headquarters! Honey – that's how it slipped through my fingers! Which of them left us a fortune? Which of them left a cent of insurance even? Only poor Jessie – one hundred to pay for her coffin. That was all, Stella! And I with my pitiful salary at the school. Yes, accuse me! Sit there and stare at me, thinking I let the place go! *I* let the place go? Where were *you*? In bed with your – Polack!

STELLA (*springing*) Blanche! You be still! That's enough! (*She starts out.*)

BLANCHE Where are you going?

STELLA I'm going into the bathroom to wash my face.

BLANCHE Oh, Stella, Stella, you're crying!

STELLA Does that surprise you?

> STELLA *goes into the bathroom. Outside is the sound of men's voices.* STANLEY, STEVE *and* MITCH *cross to the foot of the steps.*

STEVE And the old lady is on her way to Mass and she's late and there's a cop standin' in front of th' church an' she comes runnin' up an' says, "Officer – is Mass out yet?" He looks her over and says, "No, Lady, but y'r hat's on crooked!" (*They give a hoarse bellow of laughter.*)

STEVE Playing poker tomorrow night?

STANLEY Yeah – at Mitch's.

MITCH Not at my place. My mother's still sick. (*He starts off.*)

STANLEY (*calling after him*) All right, we'll play at my place...but you bring the beer.

EUNICE (*hollering down from above*) Break it up down there! I made the spaghetti dish and ate it myself.

STEVE (*going upstairs*) I told you and phoned you we was playing. (*To the men.*) Jax beer!

EUNICE You never phoned me once.

STEVE I told you at breakfast – and phoned you at lunch...

EUNICE Well, never mind about that. You just get yourself home here once in a while.

STEVE You want it in the papers?

More laughter and shouts of parting come from the men. STANLEY *throws the screen door of the kitchen open and comes in. He is of medium height, about five feet eight or nine, and strongly, compactly built. Animal joy in his being is implicit in all his movements and attitudes. Since earliest manhood the centre of his life has been pleasure with women, the giving and taking of it, not with weak indulgence, dependently, but with the power and pride of a richly feathered male bird among hens. Branching out from this complete and satisfying centre are all the auxilliary channels of his life, such as his heartiness with men, his appreciation of rough humour, his love of good drink and food and games, his car, his radio, everything that is his, that bears his emblem of the gaudy seed-bearer. He sizes women up at a glance, with sexual classifications, crude images flashing into his mind and determining the way he smiles at them.*

BLANCHE   (*drawing involuntarily back from his stare*) You must be Stanley. I'm Blanche.

STANLEY   Stella's sister?

BLANCHE   Yes.

STANLEY   H'lo. Where's the little woman?

BLANCHE   In the bathroom.

STANLEY   Oh. Didn't know you were coming in town.

BLANCHE   I – uh –

STANLEY   Where you from, Blanche?

BLANCHE   Why, I – live in Laurel.

He has crossed to the closet and removed the whisky bottle.

STANLEY   In Laurel, huh? Oh, yeah. Yeah, in Laurel, that's right. Not in my territory. Liquor goes fast in hot weather. (*He holds the bottle to the light to observe its depletion.*) Have a shot?

BLANCHE   No, I – rarely touch it.

STANLEY   Some people rarely touch it, but it touches them often.

BLANCHE   (*faintly*) Ha-ha.

STANLEY   My clothes're stickin' to me. Do you mind if I make myself comfortable? (*He starts to remove his shirt.*)

BLANCHE   Please, please do.

STANLEY   Be comfortable is my motto.

BLANCHE   It's mine, too. It's hard to stay looking fresh. I haven't washed or even powdered my face and – here you are!

STANLEY   You know you can catch cold sitting around in damp things, especially when you been exercising hard like bowling is. You're a teacher, aren't you?

BLANCHE   Yes.

STANLEY   What do you teach, Blanche?

BLANCHE   English.

STANLEY   I never was a very good English student. How long you here for, Blanche?

BLANCHE   I – don't know yet.

STANLEY   You going to shack up here?

BLANCHE   I thought I would if it's not inconvenient for you all.

STANLEY   Good.

BLANCHE   Travelling wears me out.

STANLEY   Well, take it easy.

        A cat screeches near the window. BLANCHE *springs up.*

BLANCHE   What's that?

STANLEY   Cats…Hey, Stella!

STELLA   (*faintly, from the bathroom*) Yes, Stanley.

STANLEY   Haven't fallen in, have you? (*He grins at* BLANCHE. *She tries unsuccessfully to smile back. There is a silence.*) I'm afraid I'll strike you as being the unrefined type. Stella's spoke of you a good deal. You were married once, weren't you?

The music of the polka rises up, faint in the distance.

BLANCHE   Yes. When I was quite young.

STANLEY   What happened?

BLANCHE   The boy – the boy died. (*She sinks back down.*) I'm afraid I'm – going to be sick!

Her head falls on her arms.

SCENE TWO

It is six o'clock the following evening. BLANCHE *is
bathing.* STELLA *is completing her toilette.* BLANCHE'S
dress, a flowered print, is laid out on STELLA'S *bed.*
STANLEY *enters the kitchen from outside, leaving the
door open on the perpetual "blue piano" around the
corner.*

STANLEY What's all this monkey doings?

STELLA Oh, Stan! (*She jumps up and kisses him which he
accepts with lordly composure.*) I'm taking Blanche
to Galatoires' for supper and then to a show,
because it's your poker night.

STANLEY How about my supper, huh? I'm not going to no
Galatoires' for supper!

STELLA I put you a cold plate on ice.

STANLEY Well, isn't that just dandy!

STELLA I'm going to try to keep Blanche out till the party
breaks up because I don't know how she would take
it. So we'll go to one of the little places in the Quarter
afterwards and you'd better give me some money.

STANLEY Where is she?

STELLA She's soaking in a hot tub to quiet her nerves. She's
terribly upset.

STANLEY Over what?

STELLA She's been through such an ordeal.

STANLEY Yeah?

STELLA Stan, we've – lost Belle Reve!

STANLEY The place in the country?

STELLA Yes.

STANLEY How?

STELLA (*vaguely*) Oh, it had to be – sacrificed or something.
(*There is a pause while* STANLEY *considers.* STELLA

is changing into her dress.) When she comes in be sure to say something nice about her appearance. And, oh! Don't mention the baby. I haven't said anything yet, I'm waiting until she gets in a quieter condition.

STANLEY (*ominously*) So?

STELLA And try to understand her and be nice to her, Stan.

BLANCHE (*singing from the bathroom*)

> "From the land of the sky blue water,
>   They brought a captive maid!"

STELLA She wasn't expecting to find us in such a small place. You see I'd tried to gloss things over a little in my letters.

STANLEY So?

STELLA And admire her dress and tell her she's looking wonderful. That's important to Blanche. Her little weakness!

STANLEY Yeah. I get the idea. Now let's skip back a little to where you said the country place was disposed of.

STELLA Oh! – yes…

STANLEY How about that? Let's have a few more details on that subject.

STELLA It's best not to talk much about it until she's calmed down.

STANLEY So that's the deal, huh? Sister Blanche cannot be annoyed with business details right now!

STELLA You saw how she was last night.

STANLEY Uh-hum, I saw how she was. Now let's have a gander at the bill of sale.

STELLA I haven't seen any.

STANLEY She didn't show you no papers, no deed of sale or nothing like that, huh?

STELLA It seems like it wasn't sold.

STANLEY	Well, what in hell was it then, give away? To charity?
STELLA	Shhh! She'll hear you.
STANLEY	I don't care if she hears me. Let's see the papers!
STELLA	There weren't any papers, she didn't show any papers, I don't care about papers.
STANLEY	Have you ever heard of the Napoleonic code?
STELLA	No, Stanley, I haven't heard of the Napoleonic code and if I have, I don't see what it –
STANLEY	Let me enlighten you on a point or two, baby.
STELLA	Yes?
STANLEY	In the state of Louisiana we have the Napoleonic code according to which what belongs to the wife belongs to the husband and vice versa. For instance if I had a piece of property, or you had a piece of property –
STELLA	My head is swimming!
STANLEY	All right. I'll wait till she gets through soaking in a hot tub and then I'll inquire if *she* is acquainted with the Napoleonic code. It looks to me like you have been swindled, baby, and when you're swindled under the Napoleonic code I'm swindled *too*. And I don't like to be *swindled*.
STELLA	There's plenty of time to ask her questions later but if you do it now she'll go to pieces again. I don't understand what happened to Belle Reve but you don't know how ridiculous you are being when you suggest that my sister or I or anyone of our family could have perpetrated a swindle on anyone else.
STANLEY	Then where's the money if the place was sold?
STELLA	Not sold – *lost, lost*!
	He stalks into bedroom, and she follows him.
STELLA	*Stanley*!

He pulls open the wardrobe trunk standing in middle of room and jerks out an armful of dresses.

STANLEY   Open your eyes to this stuff! You think she got them out of a teacher's pay?

STELLA   Hush!

STANLEY   Look at these feathers and furs that she come here to preen herself in! What's this here? A solid-gold dress, I believe! And this one! What is these here? Fox-pieces! (*He blows on them.*) Genuine fox fur-pieces, a half a mile long! Where are your fox-pieces, Stella? Bushy snow-white ones, no less! Where are your white fox-pieces?

STELLA   Those are inexpensive summer furs that Blanche has had a long time.

STANLEY   I got an acquaintance who deals in this sort of merchandise. I'll have him in here to appraise it. I'm willing to bet you there's thousands of dollars invested in this stuff here!

STELLA   Don't be such an idiot, Stanley!

He hurls the furs to the daybed. Then he jerks open small drawer in the trunk and pulls up a fist-full of costume jewellery.

STANLEY   And what have we here? The treasure chest of a pirate!

STELLA   Oh, Stanley!

STANLEY   Pearls! Ropes of them! What is this sister of yours, a deep-sea diver who brings up sunken treasures? Or is she the champion safe-cracker of all time! Bracelets of solid gold, too! Where are your pearls and gold bracelets?

STELLA   Shhh! Be still, Stanley!

STANLEY   And diamonds! A crown for an empress!

STELLA   A rhinestone tiara she wore to a costume ball.

STANLEY   What's rhinestone?

STELLA   Next door to glass.

STANLEY   Are you kidding? I have an acquaintance that works
           in a jewellery store. I'll have him in here to make an
           appraisal of this. Here's your plantation, or what
           was left of it, here!

STELLA   You have no idea how stupid and horrid you're
           being! Now close that trunk before she comes out
           of the bathroom!

           *He kicks the trunk partly closed and sits on the
           kitchen table.*

STANLEY   The Kowalskis and the DuBois have different
           notions.

STELLA   (*angrily*) Indeed they have, thank heavens! –
           I'm going outside. (*She snatches up her white
           hat and gloves and crosses to the outside door.*)
           You come out with me while Blanche is getting
           dressed.

STANLEY   Since when do you give me orders?

STELLA   Are you going to stay and insult her?

STANLEY   You're damn tootin' I'm going to stay here.

           STELLA *goes out on the porch.* BLANCHE *comes out of the
           bathroom in a red satin robe.*

STANLEY   That's good.

BLANCHE   (*drawing the curtains at the windows*) Excuse me
           while I slip on my pretty new dress!

STANLEY   Go right ahead, Blanche.

           She closes the drapes between the rooms.

BLANCHE   I understand there's to be a little card party to which we ladies are cordially *not* invited.

STANLEY (*ominously*) Yeah?

BLANCHE *throws off her robe and slips into a flowered print dress.*

BLANCHE Where's Stella?

STANLEY Out on the porch.

BLANCHE I'm going to ask a favour of you in a moment.

STANLEY What could that be, I wonder?

BLANCHE Some buttons in back! You may enter!

He crosses through drapes with a smouldering look.

BLANCHE How do I look?

STANLEY You look all right.

BLANCHE Many thanks! Now the buttons!

STANLEY I can't do nothing with them.

BLANCHE You men with your big clumsy fingers. May I have a drag on your cig?

STANLEY Have one for yourself.

BLANCHE Why, thanks!…It looks like my trunk has exploded.

STANLEY Me an' Stella were helping you unpack.

BLANCHE Well, you certainly did a fast and thorough job of it!

STANLEY It looks like you raided some stylish shops in Paris.

BLANCHE Ha-ha! Yes – clothes are my passion!

STANLEY What does it cost for a string of fur-pieces like that?

BLANCHE Why, those were a tribute from an admirer of mine!

STANLEY He must have had a lot of – admiration!

BLANCHE Oh, in my youth I excited some admiration. But

look at me now! (*She smiles at him radiantly.*)
Would you think it possible that I was once
considered to be – attractive?

STANLEY   Your looks are okay.

BLANCHE   I was fishing for a compliment, Stanley.

STANLEY   I don't go in for that stuff.

BLANCHE   What – stuff?

STANLEY   Compliments to women about their looks. I never
met a woman that didn't know if she was good-
looking or not without being told, and some of
them give themselves credit for more than they've
got. I once went out with a doll who said to me, "I
am the glamorous type, I am the glamorous type!" I
said, "So what?"

BLANCHE   And what did she say then?

STANLEY   She didn't say nothing. That shut her up like a
clam.

BLANCHE   Did it end the romance?

STANLEY   It ended the conversation – that was all. Some men
are took in by this Hollywood glamour stuff and
some men are not.

BLANCHE   I'm sure you belong in the second category.

STANLEY   That's right.

BLANCHE   I cannot imagine any witch of a woman casting a
spell over you.

STANLEY   That's – right.

BLANCHE   You're simple, straightforward and honest, a little bit
on the primitive side I should think. To interest you
a woman would have to – (*She pauses with an
indefinite gesture.*)

STANLEY   (*slowly*) Lay...her cards on the table.

BLANCHE   (*smiling*) Yes – yes – cards on the table...Well, life
is too full of evasions and ambiguities, I think. I like
an artist who paints in strong, bold colours, primary

colours. I don't like pinks and creams and I never cared for wishy-washy people. That was why, when you walked in here last night, I said to myself – "My sister has married a man!" – Of course that was all that I could tell about you.

STANLEY   (*booming*) Now let's cut the re-bop!

BLANCHE   (*pressing hands to her ears*) Ouuuuu!

STELLA   (*calling from the steps*) Stanley! You come out here and let Blanche finish dressing!

BLANCHE   I'm through dressing, honey.

STELLA   Well, you come out, then.

STANLEY   Your sister and I are having a little talk.

BLANCHE   (*lightly*) Honey, do me a favour. Run to the drug-store and get me a lemon-coke with plenty of chipped ice in it! – Will you do that for me, Sweetie?

STELLA   (*uncertainly*) Yes. (*She goes around the corner of the building.*)

BLANCHE   The poor thing was out there listening to us, and I have an idea she doesn't understand you as well as I do...All right; now, Mr Kowalski, let us proceed without any more double-talk. I'm ready to answer all questions. I've nothing to hide. What is it?

STANLEY   There is such a thing in this State of Louisiana as the Napoleonic code, according to which whatever belongs to my wife is also mine – and vice versa.

BLANCHE   My, but you have an impressive judicial air!

She sprays herself with her atomizer; then playfully sprays him with it. He seizes the atomizer and slams it down on the dresser. She throws back her head and laughs.

STANLEY   If I didn't know that you was my wife's sister I'd get ideas about you!

BLANCHE Such as what?

STANLEY Don't play so dumb. You know what! – Where's the papers?

BLANCHE Papers?

STANLEY Papers! That stuff that people write on!

BLANCHE Oh, papers, papers! Ha-ha! The first anniversary gift, all kinds of papers!

STANLEY I'm talking of legal papers. Connected with the plantation.

BLANCHE There *were* some papers.

STANLEY You mean they're no longer existing?

BLANCHE They probably are, somewhere.

STANLEY But not in the trunk.

BLANCHE Everything I own is in that trunk.

STANLEY Then why don't we have a look for them? (*He crosses to the trunk, shoves it roughly open and begins to open compartments.*)

BLANCHE What in the name of heaven are you thinking of! What's in the back of that little boy's mind of yours? That I am absconding with something, attempting some kind of treachery on my sister? – Let me do that! It will be faster and simpler… (*She crosses to the trunk and takes out a box.*) I keep my papers mostly in this tin box. (*She opens it.*)

STANLEY What's them underneath? (*He indicates another sheaf of paper.*)

BLANCHE These are love-letters, yellowing with antiquity, all from one boy. (*He snatches them up. She speaks fiercely.*) Give those back to me!

STANLEY I'll have a look at them first.

BLANCHE The touch of your hands insults them!

STANLEY Don't pull that stuff!

He rips off the ribbon and starts to examine them.

BLANCHE *snatches them from him, and they cascade to the floor.*

BLANCHE Now that you've touched them I'll burn them!

STANLEY (*staring, baffled*) What in hell are they?

BLANCHE (*on the floor gathering them up*) Poems a dead boy wrote. I hurt him the way that you would like to hurt me, but you can't! I'm not young and vulnerable any more. But my young husband was and I – never mind about that! Just give them back to me!

STANLEY What do you mean by saying you'll have to burn them?

BLANCHE I'm sorry, I must have lost my head for a moment. Everyone has something he won't let others touch because of their – intimate nature…

She now seems faint with exhaustion and she sits down with the strong box and puts on a pair of glasses and goes methodically through a large stack of papers.

BLANCHE Ambler & Ambler. Hmmmmm…Crabtree…More Ambler & Ambler.

STANLEY What is Ambler & Ambler?

BLANCHE A firm that made loans on the place.

STANLEY Then it *was* lost on a mortgage?

BLANCHE (*touching her forehead*) That must've been what happened.

STANLEY I don't want no ifs, ands or buts! What's all the rest of them papers?

She hands him the entire box. He carries it to the table and starts to examine the papers.

BLANCHE (*picking up a large envelope containing more papers*) There are thousands of papers, stretching back over hundreds of years, affecting Belle Reve as, piece by piece, our improvident grand-fathers and fathers and uncles and brothers exchanged the land for their epic fornications – to put it plainly! (*She removes her glasses with an exhausted laugh.*) Till finally all that was left – and Stella can verify that! – was the house itself and about twenty acres of ground, including a graveyard, to which now all but Stella and I have retreated. (*She pours the contents of the envelope on the table.*) Here all of them are, all papers! I hereby endow you with them! Take them, peruse them – commit them to memory, even! I think it's wonderfully fitting that Belle Reve should finally be this bunch of papers in your big, capable hands!...I wonder if Stella's back with my lemon-coke...

She leans back and closes her eyes.

STANLEY   I have a lawyer acquaintance who will study these out.

BLANCHE   Present them to him with a box of aspirin tablets.

STANLEY   (*becoming somewhat sheepish*) You see, under the Napoleonic code – a man has to take an interest in his wife's affairs – especially now that she's going to have a baby.

BLANCHE *opens her eyes. The "blue piano" sounds louder.*

BLANCHE   Stella? Stella going to have a baby? (*Dreamily.*) I didn't know she was going to have a baby!

She gets up and crosses to the outside door. STELLA *appears around the corner with a carton from the drug-store.* STANLEY *goes into the bedroom with the envelope and the box. The inner rooms fade to darkness and the outside wall of the house is visible.* BLANCHE *meets* STELLA *at the foot of the steps to the sidewalk.*

BLANCHE   Stella, Stella for Star! How lovely to have a baby!

(She embraces her sister. STELLA returns the embrace with a convulsive sob. BLANCHE speaks softly.) Everything is all right; we thrashed it out. I feel a bit shaky, but I think I handled it nicely. I laughed and treated it all as a joke, called him a little boy and laughed – and flirted! Yes – I was flirting with your husband, Stella!

STEVE *and* PABLO *appear carrying a case of beer.*

BLANCHE   The guests are gathering for the poker party.

The two men pass between them, and with a short, curious stare at BLANCHE, *they enter the house.*

STELLA   I'm sorry he did that to you.

BLANCHE   He's just not the sort that goes for jasmine perfume! But maybe he's what we need to mix with our blood now that we've lost Belle Reve and have to go on without Belle Reve to protect us... How pretty the sky is! I ought to go there on a rocket that never comes down.

A TAMALE VENDOR *calls out as he rounds the corner.*

VENDOR   Red hots! Red hots!

BLANCHE *utters a sharp, frightened cry and shrinks away; then she laughs breathlessly again.*

BLANCHE   Which way do we – go now – Stella?

VENDOR   Re-e-d ho-o-ot!

BLANCHE   The blind are – leading the blind!

They disappear around the corner, BLANCHE'S *desperate laughter ringing out once more. Then there is a bellowing laugh from the interior of the flat. Then the "blue piano" and the hot trumpet sound louder.*

SCENE THREE

*The Poker Night. There is a picture of Van Gogh's of
a billiard-parlour at night. The kitchen now
suggests that sort of lurid nocturnal brilliance, the
raw colours of childhood's spectrum. Over the
yellow linoleum of the kitchen table hangs an
electric bulb with a vivid green glass shade. The
poker players –* STANLEY, STEVE, MITCH *and* PABLO *–
wear coloured shirts, solid blue, a purple, a red-
and-white check, a light green, and they are men at
the peak of their physical manhood, as coarse and
direct and powerful as the primary colours. There
are vivid slices of watermelon on the table, whisky
bottles and glasses. The bedroom is relatively dim
with only the light that spills between the portières
and through the wide window on the street. For a
moment there is absorbed silence as a hand is dealt.*

STEVE   Anything wild this deal?

PABLO   One-eyed jacks are wild.

STEVE   Give me two cards.

PABLO   You, Mitch?

MITCH   I'm out.

PABLO   One.

MITCH   Anyone want a shot?

STANLEY   Yeah. Me.

PABLO   Why don't somebody go to the Chinaman's and
bring back a load of chop suey?

STANLEY   When I'm losing you want to eat! Ante up! Openers?
Openers? Get off the table, Mitch. Nothing belongs
on a poker table but cards, chips and whisky.

*He lurches up and tosses some watermelon rinds to
the floor.*

Messy, lazy
doesn't care

MITCH Kind of on your high horse, ain't you?

STANLEY How many?

STEVE Give me three.

STANLEY One.

MITCH I'm out again. I oughta go home pretty soon.

STANLEY Shut up.

MITCH I gotta sick mother. She don't go to sleep until I come in at night.

STANLEY Then why don't you stay home with her?

MITCH She says to go out, so I go out, but I don't enjoy it. All the while I keep wondering how she is.

STANLEY Aw, for God's sake, go home, then!   *uncaring*

PABLO What've you got?.

STEVE Spade flush.

MITCH You all are married. But I'll be alone when she goes. – I'm going to the bathroom.

STANLEY Hurry back and we'll fix you a sugar-tit.

MITCH Aw, lay off. (*He crosses through the bedroom into the bathroom.*)

STEVE (*dealing a hand*) Seven card stud. (*Telling his joke as he deals.*) This ole nigger is out in back of his house sittin' down th'owing corn to the chickens when all at once he hears a loud cackle and this young hen comes lickety split around the side of the house with the rooster right behind her and gaining on her fast.

STANLEY (*impatient with the story*) Deal!

STEVE But when the rooster catches sight of the nigger th'owing the corn he puts on the brakes and lets the hen get away and starts pecking corn. And the old nigger says, "Lord God, I hopes I never gits *that* hongry!"

  STEVE *and* PABLO *laugh. The sisters appear around the corner of the building.*   B45

STELLA	The game is still going on.
BLANCHE	How do I look?
STELLA	Lovely, Blanche.
BLANCHE	I feel so hot and frazzled. Wait till I powder before you open the door. Do I look done in?
STELLA	Why no. You are as fresh as a daisy.
BLANCHE	One that's been picked a few days.

STELLA *opens the door and they enter.*

STELLA	Well, well, well. I see you boys are still at it!
STANLEY	Where you been?
STELLA	Blanche and I took in a show. Blanche, this is Mr Gonzales and Mr Hubbel.
BLANCHE	Please don't get up.
STANLEY	Nobody's going to get up, so don't be worried.
STELLA	How much longer is this game going to continue?
STANLEY	Till we get ready to quit.
BLANCHE	Poker is fascinating. Could I kibitz?
STANLEY	You could not. Why don't you women go up and sit with Eunice?
STELLA	Because it is nearly two-thirty. (BLANCHE *crosses into the bedroom and partially closes the portières.*) Couldn't you call it quits after one more hand?

A chair scrapes. STANLEY *gives a loud whack of his hand on her thigh.*

| STELLA | (*sharply*) That's not fun, Stanley. |

The men laugh. STELLA *goes into the bedroom.*

STELLA	It makes me so mad when he does that in front of people.
BLANCHE	I think I will bathe.
STELLA	Again?

BLANCHE   My nerves are in knots. Is the bathroom occupied?

STELLA   I don't know.

BLANCHE knocks. MITCH opens the door and comes out, still wiping his hands on a towel.

BLANCHE   Oh! – good evening.

MITCH   Hello. (*He stares at her.*)

STELLA   Blanche, this is Harold Mitchell. My sister, Blanche DuBois.

MITCH   (*with awkward courtesy*) How do you do, Miss DuBois.

STELLA   How is your mother now, Mitch?

MITCH   About the same, thanks. She appreciated your sending over that custard. – Excuse me, please.

He crosses slowly back into the kitchen, glancing back at BLANCHE and coughing a little shyly. He realizes he still has the towel in his hands and with an embarrassed laugh hands it to STELLA. BLANCHE looks after him with a certain interest.

BLANCHE   That one seems – superior to the others.

STELLA   Yes, he is.

BLANCHE   I thought he had a sort of sensitive look.

STELLA   His mother is sick.

BLANCHE   Is he married?

STELLA   No.

BLANCHE   Is he a wolf?

STELLA   Why, Blanche? (BLANCHE *laughs.*) I don't think he would be.

BLANCHE   What does – what does he do?

She is unbuttoning her blouse.

STELLA He's on the precision bench in the spare parts department. At the plant Stanley travels for.

BLANCHE Is that something much?

STELLA No. Stanley's the only one of his crowd that's likely to get anywhere.

BLANCHE What makes you think Stanley will?

STELLA Look at him.

BLANCHE I've looked at him.

STELLA Then you should know.

BLANCHE I'm sorry, but I haven't noticed the stamp of genius even on Stanley's forehead.

She takes off her blouse and stands in her pink silk brassière and white skirt in the light through the portières. The game has continued in undertones.

STELLA It isn't on his forehead and it isn't genius.

BLANCHE Oh. Well, what is it, and where? I would like to know.

STELLA It's a drive that he has. You're standing in the light, Blanche!

BLANCHE Oh, am I?

She moves out of the yellow streak of light. STELLA *has removed her dress and put on a light blue satin kimono.*

STELLA (*with girlish laughter*) You ought to see their wives.

BLANCHE (*laughingly*) I can imagine. Big, beefy things, I suppose.

STELLA You know that one upstairs? (*More laughter.*) One time (*laughing*) the plaster – (*laughing*) cracked –

STANLEY You hens cut out that conversation in there!

STELLA You can't hear us.

STANLEY Well, you can hear me and I said to hush up!

STELLA This is my house and I'll talk as much as I want to!

BLANCHE Stella, don't start a row.

STELLA He's half drunk! – I'll be out in a minute.

She goes into the bathroom. BLANCHE *rises and crosses leisurely to a small white radio and turns it on.*

STANLEY Awright, Mitch, you in?

MITCH What? Oh! – No, I'm out!

BLANCHE *moves back into the streak of light. She raises her arms and stretches, as she moves indolently back to the chair. Rhumba music comes over the radio.* MITCH *rises at the table.*

STANLEY Who turned that on in there?

BLANCHE I did. Do you mind?

STANLEY Turn it off!

STEVE Aw, let the girls have their music.

PABLO Sure, that's good, leave it on!

STEVE Sounds like Xavier Cugat!

STANLEY *jumps up and, crossing to the radio, turns it off. He stops short at sight of* BLANCHE *in the chair. She returns his look without flinching. Then he sits again at the poker table. Two of the men have started arguing hotly.*

STEVE I didn't hear you name it.

PABLO Didn't I name it, Mitch?

MITCH I wasn't listenin'.

PABLO What were you doing, then?

STANLEY He was looking through them drapes. (*He jumps up and jerks roughly at curtains to close them.*) Now deal the hand over again and let's play cards or quit. Some people get ants when they win.

MITCH *rises as* STANLEY *returns to his seat.*

STANLEY (*yelling*) Sit down!

MITCH I'm going to the "head". Deal me out.

PABLO Sure he's got ants now. Seven five-dollar bills in his pants pocket folded as tight as spitballs.

STEVE Tomorrow you'll see him at the cashier's window getting them changed into quarters.

STANLEY And when he goes home he'll deposit them one by one in a piggy bank his mother give him for Christmas. (*Dealing.*) This game is Spit in the Ocean.

MITCH *laughs uncomfortably and continues through the portières. He stops just inside.*

BLANCHE (*softly*) Hello! The Little Boys' Room is busy right now.

MITCH We've – been drinking beer.

BLANCHE I hate beer.

MITCH It's – a hot weather drink.

BLANCHE Oh, I don't think so; it always makes me warmer. Have you got any cigs? (*She has slipped on the dark red satin wrapper.*)

MITCH Sure.

BLANCHE What kind are they?

MITCH Luckies.

BLANCHE Oh, good. What a pretty case. Silver?

MITCH Yes. Yes; read the inscription.

BLANCHE Oh, is there an inscription? I can't make it out. (*He strikes a match and moves closer.*) Oh! (*Reading with feigned difficulty.*)

> "And if God choose,
> I shall but love thee better – after – death!"

Why, that's from my favourite sonnet by Mrs Browning!

MITCH	You know it?
BLANCHE	Certainly I do!
MITCH	There's a story connected with that inscription.
BLANCHE	It sounds like a romance.
MITCH	A pretty sad one.
BLANCHE	Oh?
MITCH	The girl's dead now.
BLANCHE	(*in a tone of deep sympathy*) Oh!
MITCH	She knew she was dying when she give me this. A very strange girl, very sweet – very!
BLANCHE	She must have been fond of you. Sick people have such deep, sincere attachments.
MITCH	That's right, they certainly do.
BLANCHE	Sorrow makes for sincerity, I think.
MITCH	It sure brings it out in people.
BLANCHE	The little there is belongs to people who have experienced some sorrow.
MITCH	I believe you are right about that.
BLANCHE	I'm positive that I am. Show me a person who hasn't known any sorrow and I'll show you a shuperficial – Listen to me! My tongue is a little – thick! You boys are responsible for it. The show let out at eleven and we couldn't come home on account of the poker game so we had to go somewhere and drink. I'm not accustomed to having more than one drink. Two is the limit – and *three*! (*She laughs.*) Tonight I had three.
STANLEY	Mitch!
MITCH	Deal me out. I'm talking to Miss –
BLANCHE	DuBois.
MITCH	Miss DuBois?
BLANCHE	It's a French name. It means woods and Blanche means white, so the two together mean white woods. Like an orchard in spring! You can remember it by that.

MITCH	You're French.
BLANCHE	We are French by extraction. Our first American ancestors were French Huguenots.
MITCH	You are Stella's sister, are you not?
BLANCHE	Yes, Stella is my precious little sister. I call her little in spite of the fact that she's somewhat older than I. Just slightly. Less than a year. Will you do something for me?
MITCH	Sure. What?
BLANCHE	I bought this adorable little coloured paper lantern at a Chinese shop on Bourbon. Put it over the light bulb! Will you, please?
MITCH	Be glad to.
BLANCHE	I can't stand a naked light bulb, any more than I can a rude remark or a vulgar action.
MITCH	(*adjusting the lantern*) I guess we strike you as being a pretty rough bunch.
BLANCHE	I'm very adaptable – to circumstances.
MITCH	Well, that's a good thing to be. You are visiting Stanley and Stella?
BLANCHE	Stella hasn't been so well lately, and I came down to help her for a while. She's very run down.
MITCH	You're not –?
BLANCHE	Married? No, no. I'm an old maid schoolteacher!
MITCH	You may teach school but you're certainly not an old maid.
BLANCHE	Thank you, sir! I appreciate your gallantry!
MITCH	So you are in the teaching profession?
BLANCHE	Yes. Ah, yes…
MITCH	Grade school or high school or –
STANLEY	(*bellowing*) *Mitch*!
MITCH	*Coming*!
BLANCHE	Gracious, what lung-power…I teach high school. In Laurel.

MITCH   What do you teach? What subject?

BLANCHE   Guess!

MITCH   I bet you teach art or music? (BLANCHE *laughs delicately.*) Of course I could be wrong. You might teach arithmetic.

BLANCHE   Never arithmetic, sir; never arithmetic! (*With a laugh.*) I don't even know my multiplication tables! No, I have the misfortune of being an English instructor. I attempt to instil a bunch of bobby-soxers and drug-store Romeos with reverence for Hawthorne and Whitman and Poe!

MITCH   I guess that some of them are more interested in other things.

BLANCHE   How very right you are! Their literary heritage is not what most of them treasure above all else! But they're sweet things! And in the spring, it's touching to notice them making their first discovery of love! As if nobody had ever known it before!

The bathroom door opens and STELLA *comes out.* BLANCHE *continues talking to* MITCH.

BLANCHE   Oh! Have you finished? Wait – I'll turn on the radio.

She turns the knobs on the radio and it begins to play "Wein, Wein, nur du allein." BLANCHE *waltzes to the music with romantic gestures.* MITCH *is delighted and moves in awkward imitation like a dancing bear.* STANLEY *stalks fiercely through the portières into the bedroom. He crosses to the small white radio and snatches it off the table. With a shouted oath, he tosses the instrument out of the window.*

STELLA   *Drunk – drunk – animal thing, you!* (*She rushes* *through to the poker table.*) All of you – please go home! If any of you have one spark of decency in you –

BLANCHE (*wildly*) Stella, watch out, he's –

STANLEY *charges after* STELLA.

MEN (*feebly*) Take it easy, Stanley. Easy fellow. – Let's all…

STELLA You lay your hands on me and I'll…

She backs out of sight. He advances and disappears. There is the sound of a blow. STELLA *cries out.* BLANCHE *screams and runs into the kitchen. The men rush forward and there is grappling and cursing. Something is overturned with a crash.*

BLANCHE (*shrilly*) My sister is going to have a baby!

MITCH This is terrible.

BLANCHE Lunacy, absolute lunacy!

MITCH Get him in here men.

STANLEY *is forced, pinioned by the two men, into the bedroom. He nearly throws them off. Then all at once he subsides and is limp in their grasp. They speak quietly and lovingly to him and he leans his face on one of their shoulders.*

STELLA (*in a high, unnatural voice, out of sight*) I want to go away, I want to go away!

MITCH Poker shouldn't be played in a house with women.

BLANCHE *rushes into the bedroom.*

BLANCHE I want my sister's clothes! We'll go to that woman's upstairs!

MITCH Where is the clothes?

BLANCHE (*opening the closet*) I've got them! (*She rushes* *through to* STELLA.) Stella, Stella, precious! Dear, dear little sister, don't be afraid!

With her arms around STELLA, BLANCHE *guides her to the outside doors and upstairs.*

STANLEY (*dully*) What's the matter; what's happened?

MITCH You just blew your top, Stan.

PABLO He's okay, now.

STEVE Sure, my boy's okay!

MITCH Put him on the bed and get a wet towel.

PABLO I think coffee would do him a world of good, now.

STANLEY (*thickly*) I want water.

MITCH Put him under the shower!

The men talk quietly as they lead him to the bathroom.

STANLEY Let go of me, you sons of bitches!

Sounds of blows are heard. The water goes on full tilt.

STEVE Let's get quick out of here!

They rush to the poker table and sweep up their winnings on their way out.

MITCH (*sadly but firmly*) Poker should not be played in a house with women.

The door closes on them and the place is still. The Negro entertainers in the bar around the corner play "Paper Doll" slow and blue. After a moment STANLEY *comes out of the bathroom dripping water and still in his clinging wet polka dot drawers.*

STANLEY Stella! (*There is a pause.*) My baby doll's left me!

He breaks into sobs. Then he goes to the phone and dials, still shuddering with sobs.

STANLEY   Eunice? I want my baby! (*He waits a moment: then he hangs up and dials again.*) Eunice! I'll keep on ringin' until I talk with my baby!

An indistinguishable shrill voice is heard. He hurls phone to floor. Dissonant brass and piano sounds as the rooms dim out to darkness and the outer walls appear in the night light. The "blue piano" plays for a brief interval. Finally, STANLEY *stumbles half-dressed out to the porch and down the wooden steps to the pavement before the building. There he throws back his head like a baying hound and bellows his wife's name: "Stella! Stella, sweetheart! Stella!"*

STANLEY   Stell-*lahhhhh*!

EUNICE   (*calling down from the door of her upper apartment*) Quit that howling out there an' go back to bed!

STANLEY   I want my baby down here. Stella, Stella!

EUNICE   She ain't comin' down so you quit! Or you'll git th' law on you!

STANLEY   Stella!

EUNICE   You can't beat on a woman an' then call 'er back! She won't come! And her goin't' have a baby!...You stinker! You whelp of a Polack, you! I hope they do haul you in and turn the fire hose on you, same as the last time!

STANLEY   (*humbly*) Eunice, I want my girl to come down with me!

EUNICE   Hah! (*She slams her door.*)

STANLEY   (*with heaven-splitting violence*) *STELL-LAHHHHHH*!

The low-tone clarinet moans. The door upstairs opens again. STELLA *slips down the rickety stairs in her robe. Her eyes are glistening with tears and her hair loose about*

*her throat and shoulders. They stare at each other.
Then they come together with low, animal moans.
He falls to his knees on the steps and presses his face
to her belly, curving a little with maternity. Her eyes
go blind with tenderness as she catches his head
and raises him level with her. He snatches the
screen door open and lifts her off her feet and bears
her into the dark flat.* BLANCHE *comes out on the
upper landing in her robe and slips fearfully down
the steps.*

BLANCHE Where is my little sister? Stella? Stella?

*She stops before the dark entrance of her sister's flat.
Then catches her breath as if struck. She rushes
down to the walk before the house. She looks right
and left as if for sanctuary. The music fades away.*
MITCH *appears from around the corner.*

MITCH Miss DuBois?

BLANCHE Oh!

MITCH All quiet on the Potomac now?

BLANCHE She ran downstairs and went back in there with
him.

MITCH Sure she did.

BLANCHE I'm terrified!

MITCH Ho-ho! There's nothing to be scared of. They're
crazy about each other.

BLANCHE I'm not used to such –

MITCH Naw, it's a shame this had to happen when you just
got here. But don't take it serious.

BLANCHE Violence! Is so –

MITCH Set down on the steps and have a cigarette with me.

BLANCHE I'm not properly dressed.

MITCH That's don't make no difference in the Quarter.

BLANCHE Such a pretty silver case.

MITCH   I showed you the inscription, didn't I?

BLANCHE   Yes. (*During the pause, she looks up at the sky.*)
There's so much – so much confusion in the
world... (*He coughs diffidently.*) Thank you for
being so kind! I need kindness now.

SCENE FOUR

*It is early the following morning. There is a
confusion of street cries like a choral chant.* STELLA
*is lying down in the bedroom. Her face is serene in
the early morning sunlight. One hand rests on her
belly, rounding slightly with new maternity. From
the other dangles a book of coloured comics. Her
eyes and lips have that almost narcotized
tranquillity that is in the faces of Eastern idols. The
table is sloppy with remains of breakfast and the
debris of the preceding night, and* STANLEY'S *gaudy
pyjamas lie across the threshold of the bathroom.
The outside door is slightly ajar on a sky of summer
brilliance.* BLANCHE *appears at this door. She has
spent a sleepless night and her appearance entirely
contrasts with* STELLA'S. *She presses her knuckles
nervously to her lips as she looks through the door,
before entering.*

BLANCHE   Stella?

STELLA   (*stirring lazily*) Hmmh?

BLANCHE *utters a moaning cry and runs into the
bedroom, throwing herself down beside* STELLA *in a
rush of hysterical tenderness.*

BLANCHE   Baby, my baby sister!

STELLA   (*drawing away from her*) Blanche, what is the
matter with you?

BLANCHE *straightens up slowly and stands beside the
bed looking down at her sister with knuckles
pressed to her lips.*

BLANCHE   He's left?

STELLA   Stan? Yes.

BLANCHE	Will he be back?
STELLA	He's gone to get the car greased. Why?
BLANCHE	Why! I've been half crazy, Stella! When I found out you'd been insane enough to come back in here after what happened – I started to rush in after you!
STELLA	I'm glad you didn't.
BLANCHE	What were you thinking of? (STELLA *makes an indefinite gesture.*) Answer me! What? What?
STELLA	Please, Blanche! Sit down and stop yelling.
BLANCHE	All right, Stella. I will repeat the question quietly now. How could you come back in this place last night? Why, you must have slept with him!

STELLA *gets up in a calm and leisurely way.*

STELLA	Blanche, I'd forgotten how excitable you are. You're making much too much fuss about this.
BLANCHE	Am I?
STELLA	Yes, you are, Blanche. I know how it must have seemed to you and I'm awful sorry it had to happen, but it wasn't anything as serious as you seem to take it. In the first place, when men are drinking and playing poker anything can happen. It's always a powder-keg. He didn't know what he was doing…He was as good as a lamb when I came back and he's really very, very ashamed of himself.
BLANCHE	And that – that makes it all right?
STELLA	No, it isn't all right for anybody to make such a terrible row, but – people do sometimes. Stanley's always smashed things. Why, on our wedding night – soon as we came in here – he snatched off one of my slippers and rushed about the place smashing the light-bulbs with it.
BLANCHE	He did – *what*?

STELLA	He smashed all the light-bulbs with the heel of my slipper! (*She laughs.*)
BLANCHE	And you – you *let* him? Didn't *run*, didn't *scream*?
STELLA	I was – sort of – thrilled by it. (*She waits for a moment.*) Eunice and you had breakfast?
BLANCHE	Do you suppose I wanted my breakfast?
STELLA	There's some coffee left on the stove.
BLANCHE	You're so – matter of fact about it, Stella.
STELLA	What other can I be? He's taken the radio to get it fixed. It didn't land on the pavement so only one tube was smashed.
BLANCHE	And you are standing there smiling!
STELLA	What do you want me to do?
BLANCHE	Pull yourself together and face the facts.
STELLA	What are they, in your opinion?
BLANCHE	In my opinion? You're married to a madman!
STELLA	No!
BLANCHE	Yes, you are, your fix is worse than mine is! Only you're not being sensible about it. I'm going to *do* something. Get hold of myself and make myself a new life!
STELLA	Yes?
BLANCHE	But you've given in. And that isn't right, you're not old! You can get out.
STELLA	(*slowly and emphatically*) I'm not in anything I want to get out of.
BLANCHE	(*incredulously*) What – Stella?
STELLA	I said I am not in anything that I have a desire to get out of. Look at the mess in this room! And those empty bottles! They went through two cases last night! He promised this morning that he was going to quit having these poker parties, but you know how long such

a promise is going to keep. Oh, well, it's his
pleasure, like mine is movies and bridge. People
have got to tolerate each other's habits, I guess.

BLANCHE   I don't understand you. (STELLA *turns toward her.*) I
don't understand your indifference. Is this a
Chinese philosophy you've cultivated?

STELLA   Is what – what?

BLANCHE   This – shuffling about and mumbling – "One tube
smashed – beer-bottles – mess in the kitchen" – as
if nothing out of the ordinary has happened!
(STELLA *laughs uncertainly and picking up the
broom, twirls it in her hands.*)
Are you deliberately shaking that thing in my face?

STELLA   No.

BLANCHE   Stop it. Let go of that broom. I won't have you
cleaning up for him!

STELLA   Then who's going to do it? Are you?

BLANCHE   I? I!

STELLA   No, I didn't think so.

BLANCHE   Oh, let me think, if only my mind would function!
We've got to get hold of some money, that's the
way out!

STELLA   I guess that money is always nice to get hold of.

BLANCHE   Listen to me. I have an idea of some kind. (*Shakily
she twists a cigarette into her holder.*) Do you
remember Shep Huntleigh? (STELLA *shakes her
head.*) Of course you remember Shep Huntleigh. I
went out with him at college and wore his pin for
a while. Well –

STELLA   Well?

BLANCHE   I ran into him last winter. You know I went to
Miami during the Christmas holidays?

STELLA   No.

BLANCHE   Well, I did. I took the trip as an investment, thinking I'd meet someone with a million dollars.

STELLA   Did you?

BLANCHE   Yes. I ran into Shep Huntleigh – I ran into him on Biscayne Boulevard, on Christmas Eve, about dusk…getting into his car – Cadillac convertible; must have been a block long!

STELLA   I should think it would have been – inconvenient in traffic!

BLANCHE   You've heard of oil-wells?

STELLA   Yes – remotely.

BLANCHE   He has them, all over Texas. Texas is literally spouting gold in his pockets.

STELLA   My, my.

BLANCHE   Y'know how indifferent I am to money. I think of money in terms of what it does for you. But he could do it, he could certainly do it!

STELLA   Do what, Blanche?

BLANCHE   Why – set us up in a – shop!

STELLA   What kind of a shop?

BLANCHE   Oh, a – shop of some kind! He could do it with half what his wife throws away at the races.

STELLA   He's married.

BLANCHE   Honey, would I be here if the man weren't married? (STELLA *laughs a little.* BLANCHE *suddenly springs up and crosses to phone. She speaks shrilly.*) How do I get Western Union? – Operator! Western Union!

STELLA   That's a dial phone, honey.

BLANCHE   I can't dial, I'm too –

STELLA   Just dial O.

BLANCHE   O?

STELLA   Yes, "O" for Operator! (BLANCHE *considers a moment; then she puts the phone down.*)

BLANCHE	Give me a pencil. Where is a slip of paper? I've got to write it down first – the message, I mean…

She goes to the dressing-table, and grabs up a sheet of Kleenex and an eyebrow pencil for writing equipment.

BLANCHE Let me see now…(*She bites the pencil.*) "Darling Shep. Sister and I in desperate situation."

STELLA I beg your pardon!

BLANCHE "Sister and I in desperate situation. Will explain details later. Would you be interested in – ?" (*She bites the pencil again.*) "Would you be – interested – in…" (*She smashes the pencil on the table and springs up.*) You never get anywhere with direct appeals!

STELLA (*with a laugh*) Don't be so ridiculous, darling!

BLANCHE But I'll think of something, I've *got* to think of – *some*-thing! Don't, don't laugh at me, Stella! Please, please don't – I – I want you to look at the contents of my purse! Here's what's in it! (*She snatches her purse open.*) Sixty-five measly cents in coin of the realm!

STELLA (*crossing to bureau*) Stanley doesn't give me a regular allowance, he likes to pay bills himself, but – this morning he gave me ten dollars to smooth things over. You take five of it, Blanche, and I'll keep the rest.

BLANCHE Oh, no. No, Stella.

STELLA (*insisting*) I know how it helps your morale just having a little pocket-money on you.

BLANCHE No, thank you – I'll take to the streets!

STELLA Talk sense! How did you happen to get so low on funds?

BLANCHE Money just goes – it goes places. (*She rubs her forehead.*) Sometime today I've got to get hold of a bromo!

STELLA I'll fix you one now.

BLANCHE Not yet – I've got to keep thinking!

STELLA I wish you'd just let things go, at least for a – while…

BLANCHE Stella, I can't live with him! You can, he's your husband. But how could I stay here with him, after last night, with just those curtains between us?

STELLA Blanche, you saw him at his worst last night.

BLANCHE On the contrary, I saw him at his best! What such a man has to offer is animal force and he gave a wonderful exhibition of that! But the only way to live with such a man is to – go to bed with him! And that's your job – not mine!

STELLA After you've rested a little, you'll see it's going to work out. You don't have to worry about anything while you're here. I mean – expenses…

BLANCHE I have to plan for us both, to get us both – out!

STELLA You take it for granted that I am in something that I want to get out of.

BLANCHE I take it for granted that you still have sufficient memory of Belle Reve to find this place and these poker players impossible to live with.

STELLA Well, you're taking entirely too much for granted.

BLANCHE I can't believe you're in earnest.

STELLA No?

BLANCHE I understand how it happened – a little. You saw him in uniform, an officer, not here but –

STELLA I'm not sure it would have made any difference where I saw him.

BLANCHE Now don't say it was one of those mysterious electric things between people! If you do I'll laugh in your face.

STELLA I am not going to say anything more at all about it!

BLANCHE All right, then, don't!

STELLA	But there are things that happen between a man and a woman in the dark – that sort of make everything else seem – unimportant. (*Pause.*)
BLANCHE	What you are talking about is brutal desire – just – Desire! – the name of that rattle-trap streetcar that bangs through the Quarter, up one old narrow street and down another...
STELLA	Haven't you ever ridden on that streetcar?
BLANCHE	It brought me here. – Where I'm not wanted and where I'm ashamed to be...
STELLA	Then don't you think your superior attitude is a bit out of place?
BLANCHE	I am not being or feeling at all superior, Stella. Believe me I'm not! It's just this. This is how I look at it. A man like that is someone to go out with – once – twice – three times when the devil is in you. But live with! Have a child by?
STELLA	I have told you I love him.
BLANCHE	Then I *tremble* for you! I just – *tremble* for you...
STELLA	I can't help your trembling if you insist on trembling!
	There is a pause.
BLANCHE	May I – speak – *plainly*?
STELLA	Yes, do. Go ahead. As plainly as you want to.
	Outside, a train approaches. They are silent till the noise subsides. They are both in the bedroom. Under cover of the train's noise STANLEY *enters from outside. He stands unseen by the women, holding some packages in his arms, and overhears their following conversation. He wears an undershirt and grease-stained seersucker pants.*

BLANCHE   Well – if you'll forgive me – he's *common*!

STELLA   Why, yes, I suppose he is.

BLANCHE   Suppose! You can't have forgotten that much of our bringing up, Stella, that you just *suppose* that any part of a gentleman's in his nature! *Not one particle, no*! Oh, if he was just – *ordinary*! Just *plain* – but good and wholesome, but – *no*. There's something downright – *bestial* – about him! You're hating me saying this, aren't you?

STELLA   (*coldly*) Go on and say it all, Blanche.

BLANCHE   He acts like an animal, has an animal's habits! Eats like one, moves like one, talks like one! There's even something – sub-human – something not quite to the stage of humanity yet! Yes, something – ape-like about him, like one of those pictures I've seen in – anthropological studies! Thousands and thousands of years have passed him right by, and there he is – Stanley Kowalski – survivor of the stone age! Bearing the raw meat home from the kill in the jungle! And you – *you* here – *waiting* for him! Maybe he'll strike you or maybe grunt and kiss you! That is, if kisses have been discovered yet! Night falls and the other apes gather! There in the front of the cave, all grunting like him, and swilling and gnawing and hulking! His poker night! – you call it – this party of apes! Somebody growls – some creature snatches at something – the fight is on! *God*! Maybe we are a long way from being made in God's image, but Stella – my sister – there has been *some* progress since then! Such things as art – as poetry and music – such kinds of new light have come into the world since then! In some kinds of people some tenderer feelings have had some little beginning! That we have got to make *grow*! And *cling* to, and hold as our flag! In

this dark march toward whatever it is we're
approaching... *Don't – don't hang back with the*
brutes!

Another train passes outside. STANLEY *hesitates,*
licking his lips. Then suddenly he turns stealthily
about and withdraws through front door. The
women are still unaware of his presence. When the
train has passed he calls through the closed front
door.

STANLEY   Hey! Hey, Stella!

STELLA   (*who has listened gravely to* BLANCHE) Stanley!

BLANCHE   Stell, I –

But STELLA *has gone to the front door.* STANLEY *enters*
casually with his packages.

STANLEY   Hiyuh, Stella, Blanche back?

STELLA   Yes, she's back.

STANLEY   Hiyuh, Blanche. (*He grins at her.*)

STELLA   You must've got under the car.

STANLEY   Them darn mechanics at Fritz's don't know their
can from third base!

STELLA *has embraced him with both arms, fiercely,*
and full in the view of BLANCHE. *He laughs and*
clasps her head to him. Over her head he grins
through the curtains at BLANCHE. *As the lights fade*
away, with a lingering brightness on their embrace,
the music of the "blue piano" and trumpet and
drums is heard.

SCENE FIVE

BLANCHE *is seated in the bedroom fanning herself with a palm leaf as she reads over a just completed letter. Suddenly she bursts into a peal of laughter.* STELLA *is dressing in the bedroom.*

STELLA What are you laughing at, honey?

BLANCHE Myself, myself, for being such a liar! I'm writing a letter to Shep. (*She picks up the letter.*) "Darling Shep. I am spending the summer on the wing, making flying visits here and there. And who knows, perhaps I shall take a sudden notion to *swoop* down on *Dallas*! How would you feel about that? Ha-ha! (*She laughs nervously and brightly, touching her throat as if actually talking to* SHEP.) Forewarned is forearmed, as they say!" – How does that sound?

STELLA Uh-huh…

BLANCHE (*going on nervously*) "Most of my sister's friends go north in the summer but some have homes on the Gulf and there has been a continued round of entertainments, teas, cocktails, and luncheons – "

A disturbance is heard upstairs at the HUBBELS' *apartment.*

STELLA (*crossing to the door*) Eunice seems to be having some trouble with Steve.

EUNICE'*s voice shouts in terrible wrath.*

EUNICE I heard about you and that blonde!

STEVE That's a damn lie!

EUNICE You ain't pulling the wool over my eyes! I wouldn't mind if you'd stay down at the Four Deuces, but you always going up.

STEVE Who ever seen me up?

EUNICE I seen you chasing her 'round the balcony – I'm gonna call the vice squad!

STEVE Don't you throw that at me!

EUNICE (*shrieking*) You hit me! I'm gonna call the police!

A clatter of aluminium striking a wall is heard, followed by a man's angry roar, shouts and overturned furniture. There is a crash; then a relative hush.

BLANCHE (*brightly*) Did he *kill* her?

EUNICE *appears on the steps in daemonic disorder.*

STELLA No! She's coming downstairs.

EUNICE Call the police, I'm going to call the police! (*She rushes around the corner.*)

STELLA (*returning from the door*) Some of your sister's friends have stayed in the city.

They laugh lightly. STANLEY *comes around the corner in his green and scarlet silk bowling shirt. He trots up the steps and bangs into the kitchen.* BLANCHE *registers his entrance with nervous gestures.*

STANLEY What's a matter with Eun-uss?

STELLA She and Steve had a row. Has she got the police?

STANLEY Naw. She's gettin' a drink.

STELLA That's much more practical!

STEVE comes down nursing a bruise on his forehead and looks in the door.

STEVE *She here?*

STANLEY Naw, naw. At the Four Deuces.

STEVE That hunk! (*He looks around the corner a bit*

timidly, then turns with affected boldness and runs after her.)

BLANCHE   I must jot that down in my notebook. Ha-ha! I'm compiling a notebook of quaint little words and phrases I've picked up here.

STANLEY   You won't pick up nothing here you ain't heard before.

BLANCHE   Can I count on that?

STANLEY   You can count on it up to five hundred.

BLANCHE   That's a mighty high number. (*He jerks open the bureau drawer, slams it shut and throws shoes in a corner. At each noise* BLANCHE *winces slightly. Finally she speaks.*) What sign were you born under?

STANLEY   (*while he is dressing*) Sign?

BLANCHE   Astrological sign. I bet you were born under Aries. Aries people are forceful and dynamic. They dote on noise! They love to bang things around! You must have had lots of banging around in the army, and now that you're out, you make up for it by treating inanimate objects with such a fury!

STELLA *has been going in and out of the closet during this scene. Now she pops her head out of the closet.*

STELLA   Stanley was born just five minutes after Christmas.

BLANCHE   Capricorn – the Goat!

STANLEY   What sign were *you* born under?

BLANCHE   Oh, my birthday's next month, the fifteenth of September; that's under Virgo.

STANLEY   What's Virgo?

BLANCHE   Virgo is the Virgin.

STANLEY   (*contemptuously*) *Hah*! (*He advances a little as he knots his tie.*) Say, do you happen to know somebody named Shaw?

*Her face expresses a faint shock. She reaches for the
cologne bottle and dampens her handkerchief as she
answers carefully.*

BLANCHE   Why, everybody knows somebody named Shaw!

STANLEY   Well, this somebody named Shaw is under the
impression he met you in Laurel, but I figure he
must have got you mixed up with some other party
because this other party is someone he met at a
hotel called the Flamingo.

BLANCHE *laughs breathlessly as she touches the
cologne-dampened handkerchief to her temples.*

BLANCHE   I'm afraid he does have me mixed up with this
"other party". The Hotel Flamingo is not the sort of
establishment I would dare to be seen in!

STANLEY   You know of it?

BLANCHE   Yes, I've seen it and smelled it.

STANLEY   You must've got pretty close if you could smell it.

BLANCHE   The odour of cheap perfume is penetrating.

STANLEY   That stuff you use is expensive?

BLANCHE   Twenty-five dollars an ounce! I'm nearly out.
That's just a hint if you want to remember my
birthday! (*She speaks lightly but her voice has a note
of fear.*)

STANLEY   Shaw must've got you mixed up. He goes in and
out of Laurel all the time, so he can check on it and
clear up any mistake.

He turns away and crosses to the portières.
BLANCHE *closes her eyes as if faint. Her hand
trembles as she lifts the handkerchief again to
her forehead.* STEVE *and* EUNICE *come around the
corner.* STEVE's *arm is around* EUNICE's *shoulder
and she is sobbing luxuriously and he is cooing
love-words. There is a murmur of thunder as*

they go slowly upstairs in a tight embrace.

STANLEY   (*to* STELLA) I'll wait for you at the Four Deuces!

STELLA   Hey! Don't I rate one kiss?

STANLEY   Not in front of your sister.

He goes out. BLANCHE *rises from her chair. She seems faint; looks about her with an expression of almost panic.*

BLANCHE   Stella! What have you heard about me?

STELLA   Huh?

BLANCHE   What have people been telling you about me?

STELLA   Telling?

BLANCHE   You haven't heard any – unkind – gossip about me?

STELLA   Why, no, Blanche, of course not!

BLANCHE   Honey, there was – a good deal of talk in Laurel.

STELLA   About *you*, Blanche?

BLANCHE   I wasn't so good the last two years or so, after Belle Reve had started to slip through my fingers.

STELLA   All of us do things we –

BLANCHE   I never was hard or self-sufficient enough. When people are soft – soft people have got to court the favour of hard ones, Stella. Have got to be seductive – put on soft colours, the colours of butterfly wings, and glow – make a little – temporary magic just in order to pay for – one night's shelter! That's why I've been – not so awf'ly good lately. I've run for protection, Stella, from under one leaky roof to another leaky roof – because it was storm – all storm, and I was – caught in the centre… People don't see you – *men* don't – don't even admit your existence unless they are making love to you. And you've got to have your existence admitted by someone, if you're going to have someone's protection. And so the soft people have got to – shimmer and glow – put a –

paper lantern over the light… But I'm scared now
– awf'ly scared. I don't know how much longer I
can turn the trick. It isn't enough to be soft. You've
got to be soft *and attractive.* And I – I'm fading
now!

The afternoon has faded to dusk. STELLA *goes into
the bedroom and turns on the light under the
paper lantern. She holds a bottled soft drink in her
hand.*

Have you been listening to me?

STELLA   I don't listen to you when you are being morbid!
(*She advances with the bottled coke.*)

BLANCHE   (*with abrupt change to gaiety*) Is that coke for
me?

STELLA   Not for anyone else!

BLANCHE   Why, you precious thing, you! Is it just coke?

STELLA   (*turning*) You mean you want a shot in it!

BLANCHE   Well, honey, a shot never does a coke any harm! Let
me? You mustn't wait on me!

STELLA   I like to wait on you, Blanche. It makes it seem
more like home. (*She goes into the kitchen, finds a
glass and pours a shot of whisky into it.*)

BLANCHE   I have to admit I love to be waited on…

She rushes into the bedroom. STELLA *goes to her
with the glass.* BLANCHE *suddenly clutches* STELLA'S
*free hand with a moaning sound and presses
the hand to her lips.* STELLA *is embarrassed by her
show of emotion.* BLANCHE *speaks in a choked
voice.*

You're – you're – so *good* to me! And I –

STELLA   Blanche.

BLANCHE   I know, I won't! You hate me to talk sentimental.
But honey, *believe* I feel things more than I *tell* you!
I *won't* stay long! I won't, I *promise* I –

STELLA Blanche!

BLANCHE (*hysterically*) I won't, I promise, *I'll go! Go soon!* I will *really*! I *won't* hang around until he – throws me out...

STELLA Now will you stop talking foolish?

BLANCHE Yes, honey. Watch how you pour – that fizzy stuff foams over!

BLANCHE *laughs shrilly and grabs the glass, but her hand shakes so it almost slips from her grasp.* STELLA *pours the coke into the glass. It foams over and spills.* BLANCHE *gives a piercing cry.*

STELLA (*shocked by the cry*) Heavens!

BLANCHE Right on my pretty white skirt!

STELLA Oh...Use my hanky. Blot gently.

BLANCHE (*slowly recovering*) I know – gently – gently...

STELLA Did it stain?

BLANCHE Not a bit. Ha-ha! Isn't that lucky? (*She sits down shakily, taking a grateful drink. She holds the glass in both hands and continues to laugh a little.*)

STELLA Why did you scream like that?

BLANCHE I don't know why I scream! (*Continuing nervously.*) Mitch – Mitch is coming at seven. I guess I am just feeling nervous about our relations. (*She begins to talk rapidly and breathlessly.*) He hasn't gotten a thing but a goodnight kiss, that's all I have given him, Stella. I want his respect. And men don't want anything they get too easy. But on the other hand men lose interest quickly. Especially when the girl is over – thirty. They think a girl over thirty ought to – the vulgar term is – "put out."...And I – I'm not "putting out." Of course he – he doesn't know – I mean I haven't informed him – of my real age!

STELLA   Why are you sensitive about your age?

BLANCHE   Because of hard knocks my vanity's been given.
What I mean is – he thinks I'm sort of – prim
and proper, you know! (*She laughs out sharply.*) I
want to *deceive* him enough to make him – want
me…

STELLA   Blanche, do you want *him*?

BLANCHE   I want to *rest*! I want to breathe quietly again! Yes
– I *want* Mitch…*very badly*! Just think! If it
happens! I can leave here and not be anyone's
problem…

STANLEY *comes around the corner with a drink
under his belt.*

STANLEY   (*bawling*) Hey, Steve! Hey, Eunice! Hey, Stella!

*There are joyous calls from above. Trumpet and
drums are heard from around the corner.*

STELLA   (*kissing* BLANCHE *impulsively*) It *will* happen!

BLANCHE   (*doubtfully*) It will?

STELLA   It *will*! (*She goes across into the kitchen,
looking back at* BLANCHE.) It will, honey, *it
will*…But don't take another drink! (*Her voice
catches as she goes out of the door to meet her
husband.*)

BLANCHE *sinks faintly back in her chair with her
drink.* EUNICE *shrieks with laughter and runs down
the steps.* STEVE *bounds after her with goat-like
screeches and chases her around corner.* STANLEY
and STELLA *twine arms as they follow, laughing.
Dusk settles deeper. The music from the Four
Deuces is slow and blue.*

BLANCHE   Ah, me, ah, me, ah, me…

Her eyes fall shut and the palm leaf drops from her

fingers. She slaps her hand on the chair arm a couple of times; then she raises herself wearily to her feet and picks up the hand mirror. There is a little glimmer of lightning about the building. The NEGRO WOMAN, *cackling hysterically, swaying drunkenly, comes around the corner from the Four Deuces. At the same time, a* YOUNG MAN *enters from the opposite direction. The* NEGRO WOMAN *snaps her fingers before his belt.*

NEGRO WOMAN   Hey! Sugar!

She says something indistinguishable. The YOUNG MAN *shakes his head violently and edges hastily up the steps. He rings the bell.* BLANCHE *puts down the mirror. The* NEGRO WOMAN *has wandered down the street.*

BLANCHE   Come in.

The YOUNG MAN *appears through the portières. She regards him with interest.*

BLANCHE   Well, well! What can I do for *you?*

YOUNG MAN   I'm collecting for the *The Evening Star.*

BLANCHE   I didn't know that stars took up collections.

YOUNG MAN   It's the paper.

BLANCHE   I know, I was joking – feebly! Will you – have a drink?

YOUNG MAN   No, ma'am. No, thank you. I can't drink on the job.

BLANCHE   Oh, well, now, let's see…No, I don't have a dime! I'm not the lady of the house. I'm her sister from Mississippi. I'm one of those poor relations you've heard about.

YOUNG MAN   That's all right. I'll drop by later. (*He starts to go out. She approaches a little.*)

BLANCHE   Hey! (*He turns back shyly. She puts a cigarette in* *a long holder.*) Could you give me a light? (*She crosses toward him. They meet at the door between the two rooms.*)

YOUNG MAN Sure. (*He takes out a lighter.*) This doesn't always work.

BLANCHE It's temperamental? (*It flares.*) Ah! Thank you.

YOUNG MAN Thank *you*! (*He starts away again.*)

BLANCHE Hey! (*He turns again, still more uncertainly. She goes close to him.*) What time is it?

YOUNG MAN Fifteen of seven.

BLANCHE So late? Don't you just love these long rainy afternoons in New Orleans when an hour isn't just an hour – but a little bit of Eternity dropped in your hands – and who knows what to do with it?

YOUNG MAN Yes, ma'am.

In the ensuing pause, the "blue piano" is heard. It continues through the rest of this scene and the opening of the next. The YOUNG MAN *clears his throat and looks glancingly at the door.*

BLANCHE You – uh – didn't get wet in the shower?

YOUNG MAN No, ma'am. I stepped inside.

BLANCHE In a drug-store? And had a soda?

YOUNG MAN Uhhuh.

BLANCHE Chocolate?

YOUNG MAN No, ma'am. Cherry.

BLANCHE Mmmm!

YOUNG MAN A cherry soda!

BLANCHE You make my mouth water.

YOUNG MAN Well, I'd better be –

BLANCHE Young man! Young, young, young, young – man! Has anyone ever told you that you look like a young prince out of the Arabian Nights?

YOUNG MAN   No, ma'am.

> *The* YOUNG MAN *laughs uncomfortably and stands like a bashful kid.* BLANCHE *speaks softly to him.*

BLANCHE   Well, you do, honey lamb. Come here! Come on over here like I told you! I want to kiss you – just once – softly and sweetly on your mouth. (*Without waiting for him to accept, she crosses quickly to him and presses her lips to his.*) Run along now! It would be nice to keep you, but I've got to be good and keep my hands off children. Adios!

YOUNG MAN   Huh?

> *He stares at her a moment. She opens the door for him and blows a kiss to him as he goes down the steps with a dazed look. She stands there a little dreamily after he has disappeared. Then* MITCH *appears around the corner with a bunch of roses.*

BLANCHE   Look who's coming! My Rosenkavalier! Bow to me first! Now present them.

> *He does so. She curtsies low.*

BLANCHE   Ahhh! Merciii!

SCENE SIX

*It is about two a.m. the same night. The outer wall of
the building is visible.* BLANCHE *and* MITCH *come in.
The utter exhaustion which only a neurasthenic
personality can know is evident in* BLANCHE'*s voice
and manner.* MITCH *is solid but depressed. They have
probably been out to the amusement park on Lake
Pontchartrain, for* MITCH *is bearing, upside down, a
plaster statuette of Mae West, the sort of prize won at
shooting-galleries and carnival games of chance.*

BLANCHE (*stopping lifelessly at the steps*) Well…

MITCH *laughs uneasily.*

BLANCHE Well…

MITCH I guess it must be pretty late – and you're tired.

BLANCHE Even the hot tamale man has deserted the street,
and he hangs on till the end. (MITCH *laughs uneasily
again.*) How will you get home?

MITCH I'll walk over to Bourbon and catch an owl-car.

BLANCHE (*laughing grimly*) Is that streetcar named Desire still
grinding along the tracks at this hour?

MITCH (*heavily*) I'm afraid you haven't gotten much fun out
of this evening, Blanche.

BLANCHE I spoiled it for *you.*

MITCH No, you didn't, but I felt all the time that I wasn't
giving you much – entertainment.

BLANCHE I simply couldn't rise to the occasion. That was all. I
don't think I've ever tried to be gay and made such
a dismal mess of it. I get ten points for trying – I *did*
try.

MITCH Why did you try if you didn't feel like it, Blanche?

BLANCHE I was just obeying the law of nature.

MITCH   Which law is that?

BLANCHE   The one that says the lady must entertain the gentleman – or no dice! See if you can locate my door-key in this purse. When I'm so tired my fingers are all thumbs!

MITCH   (*rooting in her purse*) This it?

BLANCHE   No, honey, that's the key to my trunk which I must soon be packing.

MITCH   You mean you are leaving here soon?

BLANCHE   I've outstayed my welcome.

MITCH   This it?

The music fades away.

BLANCHE   Eureka! Honey, you open the door while I take a last look at the sky. (*She leans on the porch rail. He opens the door and stands awkwardly behind her.*) I'm looking for the Pleiades, the Seven Sisters, but these girls are not out tonight. Oh, yes they are, there they are! God bless them! All in a bunch going home from their little bridge party…Y'get the door open? Good boy! I guess you – want to go now…

He shuffles and coughs a little.

MITCH   Can I – uh – kiss you – good night?

BLANCHE   Why do you always ask me if you may?

MITCH   I don't know whether you want me to or not.

BLANCHE   Why should you be so doubtful?

MITCH   That night when we parked by the lake and I kissed you, you –

BLANCHE   Honey, it wasn't the kiss I objected to. I liked the kiss very much. It was the other little – familiarity – that I – felt obliged to – discourage… I didn't resent it! Not a bit in the world! In fact, I was somewhat flattered that you – desired me! But, honey, you know as well as I do that a single girl, a girl alone in the world, has got to keep a firm hold on her emotions or she'll be lost!

MITCH (*solemnly*) Lost?

BLANCHE I guess you are used to girls that like to be lost. The kind that get lost immediately, on the first date!

MITCH I like you to be exactly the way that you are, because in all my – experience – I have never known anyone like you.

BLANCHE *looks at him gravely; then she bursts into laughter and then claps a hand to her mouth.*

MITCH Are you laughing at me?

BLANCHE No, honey. The lord and lady of the house have not yet returned, so come in. We'll have a night-cap. Let's leave the lights off. Shall we?

MITCH You just – do what you want to.

BLANCHE *precedes him into the kitchen. The outer wall of the building disappears and the interiors of the two rooms can be dimly seen.*

BLANCHE (*remaining in the first room*) The other room's more comfortable – go on in. This crashing around in the dark is my search for some liquor.

MITCH You want a drink?

BLANCHE I want *you* to have a drink! You have been so anxious and solemn all evening, and so have I; we have both been anxious and solemn and now for these few last remaining moments of our lives together – I want to create – *joie de vivre*! I'm lighting a candle.

MITCH That's good.

BLANCHE We are going to be very Bohemian. We are going to pretend that we are sitting in a little artists' café on the

Left Bank in Paris! (*She lights a candle stub and puts it in a bottle.*) *Je Suis la Dame aux Camellias! Vous êtes – Armand!* Understand French?

MITCH   (*heavily*) Naw. Naw, I –

BLANCHE   *Voulez-vous couchez avec moi ce soir? Vous ne comprenez pas? Ah, quel dommage!* – I mean it's a damned good thing...I've found some liquor! Just enough for two shots without any dividends, honey...

MITCH   (*heavily*) That's – good.

She enters the bedroom with the drinks and the candle.

BLANCHE   Sit down! Why don't you take off your coat and loosen your collar!

MITCH   I better leave it on.

BLANCHE   No. I want you to be comfortable.

MITCH   I am ashamed of the way I perspire. My shirt is sticking to me.

BLANCHE   Perspiration is healthy. If people didn't perspire they would die in five minutes. (*She takes his coat from him.*) This is a nice coat. What kind of material is it?

MITCH   They call that stuff alpaca.

BLANCHE   Oh. Alpaca.

MITCH   It's very light weight alpaca.

BLANCHE   Oh. Light weight alpaca.

MITCH   I don't like to wear a wash-coat even in summer because I sweat through it.

BLANCHE   Oh.

MITCH   And it don't look neat to me. A man with a heavy build has got to be careful of what he puts on him so he don't look too clumsy.

BLANCHE   You are not too heavy.

MITCH   You don't think I am?

BLANCHE   You are not the delicate type. You have a

massive bone-structure and a very imposing
physique.

MITCH   Thank you. Last Christmas I was given a
membership to the New Orleans Athletic Club.

BLANCHE   Oh, good.

MITCH   It was the finest present I ever was given. I work out
there with the weights and I swim and I keep myself
fit. When I started there, I was getting soft in the
belly but now my belly is hard. It is so hard that
now a man can punch me in the belly and it don't
hurt me. Punch me! Go on! See? (*She pokes lightly at
him.*)

BLANCHE   Gracious. (*Her hand touches her chest.*)

MITCH   Guess how much I weigh, Blanche?

BLANCHE   Oh, I'd say in the vicinity of – one hundred and eighty?

MITCH   Guess again.

BLANCHE   Not that much?

MITCH   No. More.

BLANCHE   Well, you're a tall man and you can carry a good
deal of weight without looking awkward.

MITCH   I weigh two hundred and seventy pounds and I'm six
feet one and one half inches tall in my bare feet –
without shoes on. And that is what I weigh stripped.

BLANCHE   Oh, my goodness, me! It's awe inspiring.

MITCH   (*embarrassed*) My weight is not a very interesting
subject to talk about. (*He hesitates for a moment.*)
What's yours?

BLANCHE   My weight?

MITCH   Yes.

BLANCHE   Guess!

MITCH   Let me lift you.

BLANCHE   Samson! Go on, lift me. (*He comes behind her and
puts his hands on her waist and raises her lightly off
the ground.*) Well?

MITCH   You are light as a feather.

BLANCHE   Ha-ha! (*He lowers her but keeps his hands on her waist.* BLANCHE *speaks with an affectation of demureness.*) You may release me now.

MITCH   Huh?

BLANCHE   (*gaily*) I said unhand me, sir. (*He fumblingly embraces her. Her voice sounds gently reproving.*) Now, Mitch. Just because Stanley and Stella aren't at home is no reason why you shouldn't behave like a gentleman.

MITCH   Just give me a slap whenever I step out of bounds.

BLANCHE   That won't be necessary. You're a natural gentleman, one of the very few that are left in the world. I don't want you to think that I am severe and old maid school-teacherish or anything like that. It's just – well –

MITCH   Huh?

BLANCHE   I guess it is just that I have – old-fashioned ideals! (*She rolls her eyes, knowing he cannot see her face.* MITCH *goes to the front door. There is a considerable silence between them.* BLANCHE *sighs and* MITCH *coughs self-consciously.*)

MITCH   (*finally*) Where's Stanley and Stella tonight?

BLANCHE   They have gone out. With Mr and Mrs Hubbel upstairs.

MITCH   Where did they go?

BLANCHE   I think they were planning to go to a midnight prevue at Loew's State.

MITCH   We should all go out together some night.

BLANCHE   No. That wouldn't be a good plan.

MITCH   Why not?

BLANCHE   You are an old friend of Stanley's?

MITCH   We was together in the Two-forty-first.

BLANCHE   I guess he talks to you frankly?

MITCH   Sure.

BLANCHE Has he talked to you about me?

MITCH Oh – not very much.

BLANCHE The way you say that, I suspect that he has.

MITCH No, he hasn't said much.

BLANCHE But what he *has* said. What would you say his attitude toward me was?

MITCH Why do you want to ask that?

BLANCHE Well –

MITCH Don't you get along with him?

BLANCHE What do you think?

MITCH I don't think he understands you.

BLANCHE That is putting it mildly. If it weren't for Stella about to have a baby, I wouldn't be able to endure things here.

MITCH He isn't – nice to you?

BLANCHE He is insufferably rude. Goes out of his way to offend me.

MITCH In what way, Blanche?

BLANCHE Why, in every conceivable way.

MITCH I'm surprised to hear that.

BLANCHE Are you?

MITCH Well, I – don't see how anybody could be rude to you.

BLANCHE It's really a pretty frightful situation. You see, there's no privacy here. There's just these portières between the two rooms at night. He stalks through the rooms in his underwear at night. And I have to ask him to close the bathroom door. That sort of commonness isn't necessary. You probably wonder why I don't move out. Well, I'll tell you frankly. A teacher's salary is barely sufficient for her living-expenses. I didn't save a penny last year and so I had to come here for the summer. That's why I have to put up with my sister's

	husband. And he has to put up with me, apparently so much against his wishes...Surely he must have told you how much he hates me!
MITCH	I don't think he hates you.
BLANCHE	He hates me. Or why would he insult me? Of course there is such a thing as the hostility of – perhaps in some perverse kind of way he – No! To think of it makes me...(*She makes a gesture of revulsion. Then she finishes her drink. A pause follows.*)
MITCH	Blanche –
BLANCHE	Yes, honey?
MITCH	Can I ask you a question?
BLANCHE	Yes. What?
MITCH	How old are you?
	She makes a nervous gesture.
BLANCHE	Why do you want to know?
MITCH	I talked to my mother about you and she said, "How old is Blanche?" And I wasn't able to tell her. (*There is another pause.*)
BLANCHE	You talked to your mother about me?
MITCH	Yes.
BLANCHE	Why?
MITCH	I told my mother how nice you were, and I liked you.
BLANCHE	Were you sincere about that?
MITCH	You know I was.
BLANCHE	Why did your mother want to know my age?
MITCH	Mother is sick.
BLANCHE	I'm sorry to hear it. Badly?
MITCH	She won't live long. Maybe just a few months.
BLANCHE	Oh.
MITCH	She worries because I'm not settled.

BLANCHE	Oh.
MITCH	She wants me to be settled down before she – (*His voice is hoarse and he clears his throat twice, shuffling nervously around with his hands in and out of his pockets.*)
BLANCHE	You love her very much, don't you?
MITCH	Yes.
BLANCHE	I think you have a great capacity for devotion. You will be lonely when she passes on, won't you? (MITCH *clears his throat and nods.*) I understand what that is.
MITCH	To be lonely?
BLANCHE	I loved someone, too, and the person I loved I lost.
MITCH	Dead? (*She crosses to the window and sits on the sill, looking out. She pours herself another drink.*) A man?
BLANCHE	He was a boy, just a boy, when I was a very young girl. When I was sixteen, I made the discovery – love. All at once and much, much too completely. It was like you suddenly turned a blinding light on something that had always been half in shadow, that's how it struck the world for me. But I was unlucky. Deluded. There was something different about the boy, a nervousness, a softness and tenderness which wasn't like a man's, although he wasn't the least bit effeminate looking – still – that thing was there...He came to me for help. I didn't know that. I didn't find out anything till after our marriage when we'd run away and come back and all I knew was I'd failed him in some mysterious way and wasn't able to give the help he needed but couldn't speak of! He was in the quicksands and clutching at me – but I wasn't holding him out, I was slipping in with him! I didn't know that. I didn't know anything except I loved

him unendurably but without being able to
help him or help myself. Then I found out. In
the worst of all possible ways. By coming
suddenly into a room that I thought was empty –
which wasn't empty, but had two people in
it…

*A locomotive is heard approaching outside. She
claps her hands to her ears and crouches over. The
headlight of the locomotive glares into the room as
it thunders past. As the noise recedes she straightens
slowly and continues speaking.*

Afterwards we pretended that nothing had been
discovered. Yes, the three of us drove out to
Moon Lake Casino, very drunk and laughing all the
way.

*Polka music sounds, in a minor key faint with
distance.*

We danced the Varsouviana! Suddenly in the
middle of the dance the boy I had married broke
away from me and ran out of the casino. A few
moments later – a shot!

The Polka stops abruptly. BLANCHE *rises stiffly. Then
the Polka resumes in a major key.*

I ran out – all did! – all ran and gathered about
the terrible thing at the edge of the lake! I
couldn't get near for the crowding. Then
somebody caught my arm. "Don't go any closer!
Come back! You don't want to see!" 'See? See
what! Then I heard voices say – Allan! Allan! The
Grey boy! He'd stuck the revolver into his mouth,
and fired – so that the back of his head had been –
blown away!

She sways and covers her face.

It was because – on the dance-floor – unable to
stop myself – I'd suddenly said – "I know! I know!
You disgust me…" And then the searchlight which
had been turned on the world was turned off again
and never for one moment since has there been
any light that's stronger than this – kitchen –
candle…

MITCH *gets up awkwardly and moves towards her a
little. The Polka music increases.* MITCH *stands
beside her.*

MITCH   (*drawing her slowly into his arms*) You need
somebody. And I need somebody, too. Could it be
– you and me, Blanche?

*She stares at him vacantly for a moment. Then with
a soft cry huddles in his embrace. She makes a
sobbing effort to speak but the words won't come.
He kisses her forehead and her eyes and finally her
lips. The Polka tune fades out. Her breath is drawn
and released in long, grateful sobs.*

BLANCHE   Sometimes – there's God – so quickly!

SCENE SEVEN

*It is late afternoon in mid-September. The portières
are open and a table is set for a birthday supper,
with cake and flowers.* STELLA *is completing the
decorations as* STANLEY *comes in.*

STANLEY What's all this stuff for?

STELLA Honey, it's Blanche's birthday.

STANLEY She here?

STELLA In the bathroom.

STANLEY (*mimicking*) "Washing out some things"?

STELLA I reckon so.

STANLEY How long she been in there?

STELLA All afternoon.

STANLEY (*mimicking*) "Soaking in a hot tub"?

STELLA Yes.

STANLEY Temperature 100 on the nose, and she soaks herself
in a hot tub.

STELLA She says it cools her off for the evening.

STANLEY And you run out an' get her cokes, I suppose? And
serve 'em to Her Majesty in the tub? (STELLA *shrugs.*)
Set down here a minute.

STELLA Stanley, I've got things to do.

STANLEY Set down! I've got th' dope on your big sister, Stella.

STELLA Stanley, stop picking on Blanche.

STANLEY That girl calls *me* common!

STELLA Lately you have been doing all you can think of to
rub her the wrong way, Stanley, and Blanche is
sensitive and you've got to realize that Blanche and
I grew up under very different circumstances than
you did.

STANLEY So I been told. And told and told and told! You

know she's been feeding us a pack of lies here?

STELLA   No, I don't, and –

STANLEY   Well, she has, however. But now that cat's out of the bag! I found out some things!

STELLA   What – things?

STANLEY   Things I already suspected. But now I got proof from the most reliable sources – which I have checked on!

> BLANCHE *is singing in the bathroom a saccharine popular ballad which is used contrapunctually with* STANLEY'S *speech.*

STELLA   (*to* STANLEY) Lower your voice!

STANLEY   Some canary-bird, huh!

STELLA   Now please tell me quietly what you think you've found out about my sister.

STANLEY   Lie Number One. All this squeamishness she puts on! You should just know the line she's been feeding to Mitch. He thought she had never been more than kissed by a fellow! But Sister Blanche is no lily! Ha-ha! Some lily she is!

STELLA   What have you heard and who from?

STANLEY   Our supply-man down at the plant had been going through Laurel for years and he knows all about her and everybody else in the town of Laurel knows all about her. She is as famous in Laurel as if she was the President of the United States, only she is not respected by any party! This supply-man stops at a hotel called the Flamingo.

BLANCHE   (*singing blithely*)
"Say, it's only a paper moon, Sailing over a cardboard sea –
But it wouldn't be make-believe If you believed in me!"

STELLA   What about the – Flamingo?

STANLEY   She stayed there, too.

STELLA   My sister lived at Belle Reve.

STANLEY   This is after the home-place had slipped through her lily-white fingers! She moved to the Flamingo! A second-class hotel which has the advantage of not interfering in the private social life of the personalities there! The Flamingo is used to all kinds of goings-on. But even the management of the Flamingo was impressed by Dame Blanche! In fact they were so impressed by Dame Blanche that they requested her to turn in her room-key – for permanent! This happened a couple of weeks before she showed here.

BLANCHE   (*singing*)
"It's a Barnum and Bailey world, Just as phony as it can be –
But it wouldn't be make-believe If you believed in me!"

STELLA   What – contemptible – lies!

STANLEY   Sure, I can see how you would be upset by this. She pulled the wool over your eyes as much as Mitch's!

STELLA   It's pure invention! There's not a word of truth in it and if I were a man and this creature had dared to invent such things in my presence –

BLANCHE   (*singing*)
"Without your love,
It's a honky-tonk parade!
Without your love,
It's a melody played in a penny arcade..."

STANLEY   Honey, I told you I thoroughly checked on these stories! Now wait till I finished. The trouble with Dame Blanche was that she couldn't put on her act any more in Laurel! They got wised up after two or three dates with her and then they quit, and she goes on to another, the same old lines, same old act, same old hooey! But the town was too small for this to go on forever! And as time went by she became a town character. Regarded as not just different but downright loco – nuts.

STELLA *draws back.*

STANLEY   And for the last year or two she has been washed up like poison. That's why she's here this summer, visiting royalty, putting on all this act – because she's practically told by the mayor to get out of town! Yes, did you know there was an army camp near Laurel and your sister's was one of the places called "Out-of-Bounds"?

BLANCHE   "It's only a paper moon, just as phoney as it can be –
But it wouldn't be make-believe If you believed in me!"

STANLEY   Well, so much for her being such a refined and particular type of girl. Which brings us to Lie Number Two.

STELLA   I don't want to hear any more!

STANLEY   She's not going back to teach school! In fact I am willing to bet you that she never had no idea of returning to Laurel! She didn't resign temporarily from the high school because of her nerves! No, siree, Bob! She didn't. They kicked her out of that high school before the spring term ended – and I hate to tell you the reason that step was taken! A seventeen-year-old boy – she'd gotten mixed up with!

BLANCHE   "It's a Barnum and Bailey world, Just as phony as it can be–"

In the bathroom the water goes on loud; little breathless

cries and peals of laughter are heard as if a child were frolicking in the tub.

STELLA   This is making me – sick!

STANLEY   The boy's dad learned about it and got in touch with the high school superintendent. Boy, oh, boy, I'd like to have been in that office when Dame Blanche was called on the carpet! I'd like to have seen her trying to squirm out of that one! But they had her on the hook good and proper that time and she knew that the jig was all up! They told her she better move on to some fresh territory. Yep, it was practikly a town ordinance passed against her!

The bathroom door is open and BLANCHE *thrusts her head out holding a towel about her hair.*

BLANCHE   Stella!

STELLA   (*faintly*) Yes, Blanche?

BLANCHE   Give me another bath-towel to dry my hair with. I've just washed it.

STELLA   Yes, Blanche.

She crosses in a dazed way from the kitchen to the bathroom door with a towel.

BLANCHE   What's the matter, honey?

STELLA   Matter? Why?

BLANCHE   You have such a strange expression on your face!

STELLA   Oh – (*She tries to laugh.*) I guess I'm a little tired!

BLANCHE   Why don't you bathe, too, soon as I get out?

STANLEY   (*calling from the kitchen*) How soon is that going to be?

BLANCHE   Not so terribly long! Possess your soul in patience!

STANLEY   It's not my soul I'm worried about!

BLANCHE *slams the door.* STANLEY *laughs harshly.*
STELLA *comes slowly back into the kitchen.*

STANLEY Well, what do you think of it?

STELLA I don't believe all of those stories and I think your supply-man was mean and rotten to tell them. It's possible that some of the things he said are partly true. There are things about my sister I don't approve of – things that caused sorrow at home. She was always – flighty!

STANLEY Flighty is some word for it!

STELLA But when she was young, very young, she had an experience that – killed her illusions!

STANLEY What experience was that?

STELLA I mean her marriage, when she was – almost a child! She married a boy who wrote poetry... He was extremely good-looking. I think Blanche didn't just love him but worshipped the ground he walked on! Adored him and thought him almost too fine to be human! But then she found out –

STANLEY What?

STELLA This beautiful and talented young man was a degenerate. Didn't your supply-man give you that information?

STANLEY All we discussed was recent history. That must have been a pretty long time ago.

STELLA Yes, it was – a pretty long time ago...

STANLEY *comes up and takes her by the shoulders rather gently. She gently withdraws from him. Automatically she starts sticking little pink candles in the birthday cake.*

STANLEY How many candles are you putting in that cake?

STELLA   I'll stop at twenty-five.

STANLEY   Is company expected?

STELLA   We asked Mitch to come over for cake and ice-cream.

STANLEY *looks a little uncomfortable. He lights a cigarette from the one he has just finished.*

STANLEY   I wouldn't be expecting Mitch over tonight.

STELLA *pauses in her occupation with candles and looks slowly around at* STANLEY.

STELLA   Why?

STANLEY   Mitch is a buddy of mine. We were in the same outfit together – Two-forty-first Engineers. We work in the same plant and now on the same bowling team. You think I could face him if –

STELLA   Stanley Kowalski, did you – did you repeat what that...?

STANLEY   You're goddam right I told him! I'd have that on my conscience the rest of my life if I knew all that stuff and let my best friend get caught!

STELLA   Mitch is through with her?

STANLEY   Wouldn't you be if...?

STELLA   I said, *Is Mitch through with her?*

BLANCHE'*s voice is lifted again, serenely as a bell. She sings "But it wouldn't be make-believe If you believed in me."*

STANLEY   No, I don't think he's necessarily through with her – just wised up!

STELLA   Stanley, she thought Mitch was – going to – going to marry her. I was hoping so, too.

STANLEY   Well, he's not going to marry her. Maybe he *was,* but he's not going to jump in a tank with a school of sharks – now!

He rises.

STANLEY   Blanche! Oh, Blanche! Can I please get in my bathroom?

There is a pause.

BLANCHE   Yes, indeed, sir! Can you wait one second while I dry?

STANLEY   Having waited one hour I guess one second ought to pass in a hurry.

STELLA   And she hasn't got her job? Well, what will she do!

STANLEY   She's not stayin' here after Tuesday. You know that, don't you? Just to make sure I bought her ticket myself. A bus-ticket!

STELLA   In the first place, Blanche wouldn't go on a bus.

STANLEY   She'll go on a bus and like it.

STELLA   No, she won't, no, she won't, Stanley!

STANLEY   *She'll go!* Period. P.S. She'll go *Tuesday*!

STELLA   (*slowly*) What'll – she – do? What on earth will she – *do*!

STANLEY   Her future is mapped out for her.

STELLA   What do you mean?

BLANCHE *sings.*

STANLEY   Hey, canary bird! Toots! Get *OUT* of the *BATHROOM!* Must I speak more plainly?

The bathroom door flies open and BLANCHE *emerges with a gay peal of laughter, but as* STANLEY *crosses past her, a frightened look appears on her face, almost a look of panic. He doesn't look at her but slams the bathroom door shut as he goes in.*

BLANCHE   (*snatching up a hair-brush*) Oh, I feel so good after my long, hot bath, I feel so good and cool and – rested!

STELLA   (*sadly and doubtfully from the kitchen*) Do you, Blanche?

BLANCHE   (*brushing her hair vigorously*) Yes, I do, so refreshed. (*She tinkles her highball glass.*) A hot bath and a long, cold drink always gives me a brand new outlook on life!

She looks through the portières at STELLA, *standing between them, and slowly stops brushing.*

BLANCHE   Something has happened! – What is it?

STELLA   (*turning quickly away*) Why, nothing has happened, Blanche.

BLANCHE   You're lying! Something has!

She stares fearfully at STELLA, *who pretends to be busy at the table. The distant piano goes into a hectic breakdown.*

*gives both up and springs from the table and runs into
the next room. She clutches her throat and then runs
into the bathroom. Coughing, gagging sounds are
heard.*

STANLEY Well!

STELLA You didn't need to do that.

STANLEY Don't forget all that I took off her.

STELLA You needn't have been so cruel to someone alone as
she is.

STANLEY Delicate piece she is.

STELLA She is. She was. You don't know Blanche as a girl.
Nobody, nobody, was tender and trusting as she was.
But people like you abused her, and forced her to
change.

*He crosses into the bedroom, ripping off his shirt, and
changes into a brilliant silk bowling shirt. She follows
him.*

STELLA Do you think you're going bowling now?

STANLEY Sure.

STELLA You're not going bowling. (*She catches hold of his
shirt.*) Why did you do this to her?

STANLEY I done nothing to no one. Let go of my shirt. You've
torn it.

STELLA I want to know why first. Tell me why.

STANLEY When we first met, me and you, you thought I was
common. How right you was, baby. I was common
as dirt. You showed me the snapshot of the place
with columns. I pulled you down off them columns
and how you loved it, having them coloured lights
going! And wasn't we happy together, wasn't it all
okay till she showed here?

STELLA *makes a slight movement. Her look goes*

*suddenly inward as if some interior voice had called
her name. She begins a slow, shuffling progress from
the bedroom to the kitchen, leaning and resting on the
back of the chair and then on the edge of the table
with a blind look and listening expression.* STANLEY,
finishing with his shirt, is unaware of her reaction.

And wasn't we happy together! Wasn't it all okay? Till
she showed here. Hoity-toity, describing me as an
ape. (*He suddenly notices the change in* STELLA.) Hey,
what is it, Stel? (*He crosses to her.*)

STELLA   (*quietly*) Take me to the hospital.

*He is with her now, supporting her with his arm,
murmuring indistinguishably as they go outside. The
"Varsouviana" is heard, its music rising with sinister
rapidity as the bathroom door opens slightly.* BLANCHE
*comes out twisting a washcloth. She begins to whisper
the words as the light fades slowly.*

BLANCHE   *El pan de mais, el pan de mais,
El pan de mais, sin sal.
El pan de mais, el pan de mais,
El pan de mais sin sal…*

SCENE NINE

Acting an like queen

A while later that evening. BLANCHE *is seated in a tense hunched position in a bedroom chair that she has recovered with diagonal green and white stripes. She has on her scarlet satin robe. On the table beside the chair is a bottle of liquor and a glass. The rapid, feverish polka tune, the "Varsouviana", is heard. The music is in her mind; she is drinking to escape it and the sense of disaster closing in on her, and she seems to whisper the words of the song. An electric fan is turning back and forth across her.*

Drinking to get rid of Sorrow

MITCH *comes around the corner in work cloths: blue denim shirt and pants. He is unshaven. He climbs the steps to the door and rings,* BLANCHE *is startled.*

BLANCHE Who is it, please?

MITCH (*hoarsely*) Me. Mitch.

The polka tune stops.

BLANCHE Mitch! – Just a minute.

She rushes about frantically, hiding the bottle in a closet, crouching at the mirror and dabbing her face with cologne and powder. She is so excited that her breath is audible as she dashes about. At last she rushes to the door in the kitchen and lets him in.

BLANCHE Mitch! – Y'now, I really shouldn't let you in after the treatment I have received from you this evening! So utterly uncavalier! But hello, beautiful!

Acting like queen again

She offers him her lips. He ignores it and pushes past

*her into the flat. She looks fearfully after him as he
stalks into the bedroom.*

BLANCHE My, my, what a cold shoulder! And a face like a
thundercloud! And such <u>uncouth apparel!</u> Why, you
haven't even shaven! The unforgivable insult to a
lady! But I forgive you. I forgive you because it's such
a relief to see you. You've stopped that polka tune
that I had caught in my head. Have you ever had
anything caught in your head? Some words, a piece
of music? That goes relentlessly on and on in your
head? No, of course you haven't, you <u>dumb angel-
puss,</u> you'd never get anything awful caught in your
head!

*He stares at her while she follows him while she talks.
It is obvious that he has had a few drinks on the way
over.*

MITCH Do we have to have the fan on?

BLANCHE No!

MITCH I don't like fans.

BLANCHE Then let's turn it off, honey. I'm not partial to them!

*She presses the switch and the fan nods slowly off. She
clears her throat uneasily as* MITCH *plumps himself
down on the bed in the bedroom and lights a
cigarette.*

BLANCHE I don't know what there is to drink. I – haven't
investigated.

MITCH I don't want Stan's liquor.

BLANCHE It isn't Stan's. Everything here isn't Stan's. Some things
on the premises are actually mine! How is your
mother? Isn't your mother well?

MITCH Why?

BLANCHE Something's the matter tonight, but never mind. I
won't <u>cross-examine the witness.</u> I'll just – (*She touches*

*her forehead vaguely. The polka tune starts up
again.)* – pretend I don't notice anything different
about you! That – music again...

MITCH   What music? *Obsessed by music.
More caught up with music
than mitch.*

BLANCHE   The "Varsouvania"? The polka tune they were
playing when Allan – Wait!

A distant revolver shot is heard. BLANCHE *seems
relieved.*

BLANCHE   There now, the shot! It always stops after that.

The polka tune music dies out again.

BLANCHE   Yes, now it's stopped.

MITCH   Are you boxed out of your mind? *Drunk*

BLANCHE   I'll go and see what I can find in the way of – (*She
crosses into the closet, pretending to search for a
bottle.*) Oh, by the way, excuse me for not being
dressed. But I'd practically given you up! Had you
forgotten your invitation to supper?

MITCH   I wasn't going to see you any more.

BLANCHE   Wait a minute. I can't hear what you're saying and
you talk so little that when you do say something, I
don't want to miss a single syllable of it... What am I
looking around here for? Oh, yes – liquor! We've
had so much excitement around here this evening
that I *am* boxed out of my mind! (*She pretends
suddenly to find the bottle. He draws his foot up on
the bed and stares at her contemptuously.*) Here's
something. Southern Comfort! What is that, I
wonder?

MITCH   If you don't know, it must belong to Stan.

BLANCHE   Take your foot off the bed. It has a light cover on
it. Of course you boys don't notice things like that.
I've done so much with this place since I've been
here. *Trying to feel at home
in control*

MITCH   I bet you have.

BLANCHE   You saw it before I came. Well, look at it now! This room is almost – dainty! I want to keep it that way. I wonder if this stuff ought to be mixed with something? Ummm, it's sweet, so sweet! It's terribly, terribly sweet! Why, it's a *liqueur*, I believe! Yes, that's what it *is,* a liqueur! (MITCH *grunts.*) I'm afraid you won't like it, but try it, and maybe you will.

MITCH   I told you already I don't want none of his liquor and I mean it. You ought to lay off his liquor. He says you been lapping it up all summer like a wild-cat!

BLANCHE   What a fantastic statement! Fantastic of him saying it, fantastic of you to repeat it! I won't descend to the level of such cheap accusations to answer them, even!

[handwritten margin note: Talk down og. Putting herself a pedi]

MITCH   Huh.

BLANCHE   What's in your mind? I see something in your eyes!

MITCH   (*getting up*) It's dark in here.

BLANCHE   I like it dark. The dark is comforting to me.

MITCH   I don't think I ever seen you in the light. (BLANCHE *laughs breathlessly.*) That's a fact!

[handwritten margin note: Ashamed of herself.]

BLANCHE   Is it?

MITCH   I've never seen you in the afternoon.

BLANCHE   Whose fault is that?

MITCH   You never go out in the afternoon.

BLANCHE   Why, Mitch, you're at the plant in the afternoon!

MITCH   Not Sunday afternoon. I've asked you to go out with me sometimes on Sundays but you always make an excuse. You never want to go out till six and then it's always some place that's not lighted much.

BLANCHE   There is some obscure meaning in this but I fail to catch it.

MITCH What it means is I've never had a real look at you, Blanche.

BLANCHE What are you leading up to?

MITCH Let's turn the light on here.

BLANCHE (*fearfully*) Light? Which light? What for?

MITCH This one with the paper thing on it. (*He tears the paper lantern off the light bulb. She utters a frightened gasp.*) *[handwritten: Harsh light / reality over Blanche]*

BLANCHE What did you do that for?

MITCH So I can take a look at you good and plain!

BLANCHE Of course you don't really mean to be insulting!

MITCH No, just realistic.

BLANCHE I don't want realism.

MITCH Naw, I guess not.

BLANCHE I'll tell you what I want. Magic! (MITCH *laughs.*) Yes, yes, magic! I try to give that to people. I misrepresent things to them. I don't tell the truth, I tell what *ought* to be the truth. And if that is sinful, then let me be damned for it! – *Don't turn the light on!*

[handwritten left margin: Telling about her life & what she has done. Lied]

MITCH *crosses to the switch. He turns the light on and stares at her. She cries out and covers her face. He turns the light off again.*

MITCH (*slowly and bitterly*) I don't mind you being older than what I thought. But the rest of it – God! That pitch about your ideals being so old-fashioned and all the malarky that you've dished out all summer. Oh, I knew you weren't sixteen any more. But I was a fool enough to believe you was straight. *[handwritten: Honest.]*

BLANCHE Who told you I wasn't – "straight"? My loving brother-in-law. And you believed him.

MITCH I called him a liar at first. And then I checked on the story. First I asked our supply-man who travels through

Laurel. And then I talked directly over long-distance to this merchant.

BLANCHE   Who is the merchant?

MITCH   Kiefaber.

BLANCHE   The merchant Kiefaber of Laurel! I know the man. He whistled at me. I put him in his place. So now for revenge he makes up stories about me.

MITCH   Three people, Kiefaber, Stanley and Shaw, swore to them!

BLANCHE   Rub-a-dub-dub, three men in a tub! And such a filthy tub!

MITCH   Didn't you stay at a hotel called The Flamingo?

BLANCHE   Flamingo? No! Tarantula was the name of it! I stayed at a hotel called The Tarantula Arms!

MITCH   (*stupidly*) Tarantula?

BLANCHE   Yes, a big spider! That's where I brought my victims. (*She pours herself another drink.*) Yes, I had many intimacies with strangers. After the death of Allan – the intimacies with strangers was all I seemed able to fill my empty head with…I think it was panic, just panic, that drove me from one to another, hunting for some protection – here and there, in the most – unlikely places – even, at last, in a seventeen-year-old boy but – somebody wrote the superintendent about it – "This woman is morally unfit for her position!"

She throws back her head with convulsive, sobbing laughter. Then she repeats the statement, gasps, and drinks.

BLANCHE   True? Yes, I suppose – unfit somehow – anyway…So I came here. There was nowhere else I could go. I was played out. You know what played out is? My youth was suddenly gone up the water-spout, and

– I met you. You said you needed somebody.
Well, I needed somebody, too. I thanked God for
you, because you seemed to be gentle – a cleft in
the rock of the world that I could hide in! The
poor man's Paradise – is a little peace...But I guess
I was asking, hoping – too much! Kiefaber, Stanley
and Shaw have tied an old tin can to the tail of the
kite.

There is a pause. MITCH *stares at her dumbly.*

MITCH   You lied to me, Blanche.

BLANCHE   Don't say I lied to you.

MITCH   Lies, lies, inside and out, all lies.

BLANCHE   Never inside, I didn't lie in my heart...

A vendor comes around the corner. She is a blind
MEXICAN WOMAN *in a dark shawl, carrying bunches
of gaudy tin flowers that lower class Mexicans
display at funerals and other festival occasions. She
is calling barely audibly. Her figure is only faintly
visible outside the building.*

MEXICAN WOMAN   *Flores. Flores. Flores para los muertos –
Flores. Flores.*

BLANCHE   What? Oh! Somebody outside...I – I lived in a
house where dying old women remembered their
dead men...

MEXICAN WOMAN   *Flores. Flores para los muertos...*

The polka tune fades in.

BLANCHE   (*as if to herself*) Crumble and fade and – regrets –
recriminations... "If you'd done this, it wouldn't've
cost me that!"

MEXICAN WOMAN   *Corones pasra los muertos. Corones...*

BLANCHE   Legacies! Huh ... And other things such as

blood-stained pillow-slips – "Her linen needs changing" – "Yes Mother. But couldn't we get a coloured girl to do it?" No, we couldn't of course. Everything gone but the...

MEXICAN WOMAN   *Flores.*

BLANCHE   Death – I used to sit here and she used to sit over there and death was as close as you are... We didn't dare even admit we had ever heard of it!

MEXICAN WOMAN   *Flores para los muertos, flores – flores...*

BLANCHE   The opposite is desire. So do you wonder? How could you possibly wonder! Not far from Belle Reve, before we had lost Belle Reve, was a camp where they trained young soldiers. On Saturday nights they would go in town to get drunk...

MEXICAN WOMAN   (*softly*) *Corones...*

BLANCHE   – and on the way back they would stagger on to my lawn and call – "Blanche! Blanche!" – the deaf old lady remaining suspected nothing. But sometimes I slipped outside to answer their calls ... Later the paddy-wagon would gather them up like daisies...the long way home...

The MEXICAN WOMAN *turns slowly and drifts back off with her soft mournful cries.* BLANCHE *goes to the dresser and leans forward on it. After a moment,* MITCH *rises and follows her purposefully. The polka music fades away. He places his hands on her waist and tries to turn her about.*

BLANCHE   What do you want?

MITCH   (*fumbling to embrace her*) What I been missing all summer.

BLANCHE   Then marry me, Mitch!

MITCH   I don't think I want to marry you any more.

BLANCHE   No?

MITCH   (*dropping his hands from her waist*) You're not
          clean enough to bring in the house with my
          mother.

BLANCHE   Go away, then. (*He stares at her.*) Get out of here
          quick before I start screaming fire! (*Her throat is
          tightening with hysteria.*) Get out of here quick
          before I start screaming fire.

          *He still remains staring. She suddenly rushes to the
          big window with its pale blue square of the soft
          summer light and cries wildly.*

          Fire! Fire! Fire!

          With a startled gasp, MITCH *turns and goes out of the
          outer door, clatters awkwardly down the steps and
          around the corner of the building.* BLANCHE *staggers
          back from the window and falls to her knees. The
          distant piano is slow and blue.*

SCENE TEN

It is a few hours later that night. BLANCHE *has been
drinking fairly steadily since* MITCH *left. She has
dragged her wardrobe trunk into the centre of the
bedroom. It hangs open with flowery dresses thrown
across it. As the drinking and packing went on, a
mood of hysterical exhilaration came into her and
she has decked herself out in a somewhat soiled
and crumpled white satin evening gown and a pair
of scuffed silver slippers with brilliants set in their
heels. Now she is placing the rhinestone tiara on her
head before the mirror of the dressing-table and
murmuring excitedly as if to a group of spectral
admirers.*

BLANCHE How about taking a swim, a moonlight swim at the
old rock-quarry? If anyone's sober enough to drive
a car! Ha-ha! Best way in the world to stop your
head buzzing! Only you've got to be careful to
dive where the deep pool is – if you hit a rock you
don't come up till tomorrow…

*Tremblingly she lifts the hand mirror for a closer
inspection. She catches her breath and slams the
mirror face down with such violence that the glass
cracks. She moans a little and attempts to rise.*
STANLEY *appears around the corner of the building.
He still has on the vivid green silk bowling shirt. As
he rounds the corner the honky-tonk music is
heard. It continues softly throughout the scene. He
enters the kitchen, slamming the door. As he peers
in at* BLANCHE, *he gives a low whistle. He has had a
few drinks on the way and has brought some quart
beer bottles home with him.*

BLANCHE How is my sister?

STANLEY	She is doing okay.
BLANCHE	And how is the baby?
STANLEY	(*grinning amiably*) The baby won't come before morning so they told me to go home and get a little shut-eye.
BLANCHE	Does that mean we are to be alone in here?
STANLEY	Yep. Just me and you, Blanche. Unless you got somebody hid under the bed. What've you got on those fine feathers for?
BLANCHE	Oh, that's right. You left before my wire came.
STANLEY	You got a wire?
BLANCHE	I received a telegram from an old admirer of mine.
STANLEY	Anything good?
BLANCHE	I think so. An invitation.
STANLEY	What to? A fireman's ball?
BLANCHE	(*throwing back her head*) A cruise of the Caribbean on a yacht!
STANLEY	Well, well. What do you know?
BLANCHE	I have never been so surprised in my life.
STANLEY	I guess not.
BLANCHE	It came like a bolt from the blue!
STANLEY	Who did you say it was from?
BLANCHE	An old beau of mine.
STANLEY	The one that give you the white fox-pieces?
BLANCHE	Mr Shep Huntleigh. I wore his ATO pin my last year at college. I hadn't seen him again until last Christmas. I ran in to him on Biscayne Boulevard. Then – just now – a wire – inviting me on a cruise of the Caribbean! The problem is clothes. I tore into my trunk to see what I have that's suitable for the tropics!
STANLEY	And come up with that – gorgeous – diamond – tiara?

[handwritten margin note: Auxiliary Territorial Officer]

[handwritten left margin: world]

BLANCHE   This old relic! Ha-ha! It's only rhinestones. *Knows its not so special.*

STANLEY   Gosh. I thought it was Tiffany diamonds. (*He unbuttons his shirt.*) *Expensive jewelers in NY (USA)*

BLANCHE   Well, anyhow, I shall be entertained in style.

STANLEY   Uh-huh. It goes to show, you never know what is coming.

BLANCHE   Just when I thought my luck had begun to fail me…

STANLEY   Into the picture pops this Miami millionaire.

BLANCHE   This man is not from Miami. This man is from Dallas.

STANLEY   This man is from Dallas?

BLANCHE   Yes, this man is from Dallas where gold spouts out of the ground!

STANLEY   Well, just so he's from somewhere! (*He starts removing his shirt.*)

BLANCHE   Close the curtains before you undress any further.

STANLEY   (*amiably*) This is all I'm going to undress right now. (*He rips the sack of quart beer-bottles.*) Seen a bottle-opener?

She moves slowly towards the dresser, where she stands with her hands knotted together.

STANLEY   I used to have a cousin who could open a beer-bottle with his teeth. (*Pounding the bottle cap on the corner of the table.*) That was his only accomplishment, all he could do – he was just a human bottle-opener. And then one time, at a wedding party, he broke his front teeth off! After that he was so ashamed of himself he used t' sneak out of the house when company came…

Manly

The bottle cap pops off and a geyser of foam shoots up.
STANLEY *laughs happily, holding up the bottle over his*

head.

Ha-ha! Rain from heaven! (*He extends the bottle towards her.*) Shall we bury the hatchet and make it a loving-cup? Huh?

BLANCHE No, thank you.

STANLEY Well, it's a red letter night for us both. You having an oil-millionaire and me having a baby.

He goes to the bureau in the bedroom and crouches to remove something from the bottom drawer.

BLANCHE (*drawing back*) What are you doing in here?

STANLEY Here's something I always break out on special occasions like this! The silk pyjamas I wore on my wedding night!

BLANCHE Oh.

STANLEY When the telephone rings and they say, "You've got a son!" I'll tear this off and wave it like a flag! (*He shakes out a brilliant pyjama coat.*) I guess we are both entitled to put on the dog. (*He goes back to the kitchen with the coat over his arm.*)

BLANCHE When I think of how divine it is going to be to have such a thing as privacy once more – I would weep with joy!

STANLEY This millionaire from Dallas is not going to interfere with your privacy any?

BLANCHE It won't be the sort of thing you have in mind. This man is a gentleman and he respects me. (*Improvising feverishly.*) What he wants is my companionship. Having great wealth sometimes makes people lonely!

STANLEY I wouldn't know about that.

BLANCHE A cultivated woman, a woman of intelligence and breeding, can enrich a man's life – immeasurably! I have those things to offer, and this doesn't take them away. Physical beauty is passing. A transitory possession. But beauty of the mind and richness of the spirit and tenderness of the heart – and I have all of those things – aren't taken away, but grow! Increase with the years! How strange that I should be called a destitute woman! When I have all of these treasures locked in my heart. (*A choked sob comes from her.*) I think of myself as a very, very rich woman! But I have been foolish – casting my pearls before swine!   *Wasting potential*

STANLEY   Swine, huh?

BLANCHE   Yes, swine! Swine! And I'm thinking not only of you but of your friend, Mr Mitchell. He came to see me tonight. He dared to come here in his work-clothes! And to repeat slander to me, vicious stories that he had gotten from you! I gave him his walking papers...

STANLEY   You did, huh?

BLANCHE   But then he came back. He returned with a box of roses to beg my forgiveness. He implored my forgiveness. But some things are not forgivable. Deliberate cruelty is not forgivable. It is the one unforgivable thing in my opinion and it is the one thing of which I have never, never been guilty. And so I told him, I said to him, "Thank you," but it was foolish of me to think that we could ever adapt ourselves to each other. Our ways of life are too different. Our attitudes and our backgrounds are incompatible. We have to be realistic about such things. So farewell, my friend! And let there be no hard feelings...

STANLEY   Was this before or after the telegram came from the Texas oil millionaire?

BLANCHE   What telegram? No! No, after! As a matter of fact, the wire came just as –

STANLEY   As a matter of fact there wasn't no wire at all!

BLANCHE   Oh, oh!

STANLEY   There isn't no millionaire! And Mitch didn't come back with roses 'cause I know where he is –

BLANCHE   Oh!

STANLEY   There isn't a goddamn thing but imagination!

BLANCHE   Oh!

STANLEY   And lies and conceit and tricks!

BLANCHE   Oh!

STANLEY   And look at yourself! Take a look at yourself in that worn-out Mardi Gras outfit, rented for fifty cents from some rag-picker! And with the crazy crown on! What queen do you think you are!

BLANCHE   Oh – God...

STANLEY   I've been on to you from the start! Not once did you pull any wool over this boy's eyes! You come in here and sprinkle the place with powder and spray perfume and cover the light-bulb with a paper lantern, and lo and behold the place has turned into Egypt and you are the Queen of the Nile! Sitting on your throne and swilling down my liquor! I say – *Ha – Ha!* Do you hear me? *Ha – ha – ha!* (*He walks into the bedroom.*)

BLANCHE   Don't come in here!

Lurid reflections appear on the walls around BLANCHE. *The shadows are of a grotesque and menacing form. She catches her breath, crosses to the phone and jiggles the hook.* STANLEY *goes into the bathroom and closes the door.*

BLANCHE   Operator, operator! Give me long-distance, please...I want to get in touch with Mr Shep Huntleigh of Dallas. He's so well-known he doesn't require any address. Just ask anybody who – Wait! – No, I couldn't find it right now...Please understand, I –

No! No, wait!…One moment! Someone is –
Nothing! Hold on, please!

*She sets the phone down and crosses warily into
the kitchen. The night is filled with inhuman
voices like cries in a jungle. The shadows and
lurid reflections move sinuously as flames along
the wall spaces. Through the back wall of the
rooms, which have become transparent, can be
seen the sidewalk. A prostitute has rolled a
drunkard. He pursues her along the walk, overtakes
her and there is a struggle. A policeman's whistle
breaks it up. The figures disappear. Some moments
later the* NEGRO WOMAN *appears around the corner
with a sequinned bag which the prostitute had
dropped on the walk. She is rooting excitedly
through it.* BLANCHE *presses her knuckles to her lips
and returns slowly to the phone. She speaks in a
hoarse whisper.*

Operator! Operator! Never mind long-distance. Get
Western Union. There isn't time to be – Western –
Western Union!

She waits anxiously.

Western Union? Yes! I – want to – Take down
this message! "In desperate, desperate
circumstances! Help me! Caught in a trap. Caught
in –" *Oh!*

The bathroom door is thrown open and STANLEY
*comes out in the brilliant silk pyjamas. He grins
at her as he knots the tasselled sash about his waist.
She gasps and backs away from the phone. He
stares at her for a count of ten. Then a clicking
becomes audible from the telephone, steady and
rasping.*

STANLEY   You left th' phone off th' hook.

He crosses to it deliberately and sets it back on the hook. After he has replaced it, he stares at her again, his mouth slowly curving into a grin, and he waves between BLANCHE *and the outer door. The barely audible "blue piano" begins to drum up louder. The sound of it turns into the roar of an approaching locomotive.* BLANCHE *crouches, pressing her fists to her ears until it has gone by.*

BLANCHE (*finally straightening*) Let me – let me get by you!

STANLEY Get by me? Sure. Go ahead. (*He moves back a pace in the doorway.*)

BLANCHE You – you stand over there! (*She indicates a further position.*)

STANLEY (*grinning*) You got plenty of room to walk by me now.

BLANCHE Not with you there! But I've got to get out somehow!

STANLEY You think I'll interfere with you? Ha-ha!

The "blue piano" goes softly. She turns confusedly and makes a faint gesture. The inhuman jungle voices rise up. He takes a step towards her, biting his tongue which protrudes between his lips.

(*softly*) Come to think of it – maybe you wouldn't be bad to – interfere with...

BLANCHE *moves backward through the door into the bedroom.*

BLANCHE Stay back! Don't you come towards me another step or I'll...

STANLEY What?

BLANCHE Some awful thing will happen! It will!

STANLEY What are you putting on now?

They are now both inside the bedroom.

BLANCHE I warn you, don't, I'm in danger!

He takes another step. She smashes a bottle on the table and faces him, clutching the broken top.

STANLEY What did you do that for?

BLANCHE So I could twist the broken end in your face!

STANLEY I bet you would do that!

BLANCHE I would! I will if you…

STANLEY Oh! So you want some rough-house! All right, let's have some rough-house!

He springs towards her, overturning the table. She cries out and strikes at him with the bottle top but he catches her wrist.

Tiger – tiger! Drop the bottle-top! Drop it! We've had this date with each other from the beginning!

She moans. The bottle-top falls. She sinks to her knees. He picks up her inert figure and carries her to the bed. The hot trumpet and drums from the Four Deuces sound loudly.

SCENE ELEVEN

It is some weeks later. STELLA *is packing* BLANCHE'S
*things. Sounds of water can be heard running in
the bathroom. The portières are partly open on the
poker players –* STANLEY, STEVE, MITCH *and* PABLO *–
who sit around the table in the kitchen. The
atmosphere of the kitchen is now the same raw,
lurid one of the disastrous poker night. The building
is framed by the sky of turquoise.* STELLA *has been
crying as she arranges the flowery dresses in the
open trunk.* EUNICE *comes down the steps from her
flat above and enters the kitchen. There is another
burst from the poker table.*

STANLEY   Drew to an inside straight and made it, by God.

PABLO   *Maldita sea tu suerto!*

STANLEY   Put it in English, greaseball.

PABLO   I am cursing your goddamn luck.

STANLEY   (*prodigiously elated*) You know what luck is? Luck
is believing you're lucky. Take at Salerno. I
believed I was lucky. I figured that 4 out of 5
would not come through but I would...and I did. I
put that down as a rule. To hold front position in
this rat-race you've got to believe you are lucky.

MITCH   You...you...you...Brag...brag...bull...bull.

     STELLA *goes into the bedroom and starts folding a
dress.*

STANLEY   What's the matter with him?

EUNICE   (*walking past the table*) I always did say that
men are callous things with no feelings, but
this does beat anything. Making pigs of
yourselves. (*She comes through the portières*

into the bedroom.)

STANLEY   What's the matter with her?

STELLA   How is my baby!

EUNICE   Sleeping like a little angel. Brought you some grapes. (*She puts them on a stool and lowers her voice*.) Blanche?

STELLA   Bathing.

EUNICE   How is she?

STELLA   She wouldn't eat anything but asked for a drink.

EUNICE   What did you tell her?

STELLA   I – just told her that – we'd made arrangements for her to rest in the country. She's got it mixed in her mind with Shep Huntleigh.

BLANCHE *opens the bathroom door slightly*.

BLANCHE   Stella.

STELLA   Yes, Blanche?

BLANCHE   If anyone calls while I'm bathing take the number and tell them I'll call right back.

STELLA   Yes.

BLANCHE   That cool yellow silk – the bouclé. See if it's crushed. If it's not too crushed I'll wear it and on the lapel that silver and turquoise pin in the shape of a seahorse. You will find them in the heart-shaped box I keep my accessories in. And Stella…Try and locate a bunch of artificial violets in that box, too, to pin with the seahorse on the lapel of the jacket.

She closes the door. STELLA *turns to* EUNICE.

STELLA   I don't know if I did the right thing.

EUNICE   What else could you do?

STELLA   I couldn't believe her story and go on living with Stanley.

EUNICE   Don't ever believe it. Life has got to go on. No matter what happens, you've got to keep on going.

The bathroom door opens a little.

BLANCHE   (*looking out*) Is the coast clear?

STELLA   Yes, Blanche. (*To* EUNICE.) Tell her how well she's looking.

BLANCHE   Please close the curtains before I come out.

STELLA   They're closed.

STANLEY   – How many for you.

PABLO   Two. –

STEVE   – Three.

BLANCHE *appears in the amber light of the door. She has a tragic radiance in her red satin robe following the sculptural lines of her body. The "Varsouviana" rises audibly as* BLANCHE *enters the bedroom.*

BLANCHE   (*with faintly hysterical vivacity*) I have just washed my hair.

STELLA   Did you?

BLANCHE   I'm not sure I got the soap out.

EUNICE   Such fine hair!

BLANCHE   (*accepting the compliment*) It's a problem. Didn't I get a call?

STELLA   Who from, Blanche?

BLANCHE   Shep Huntleigh…

STELLA   Why, not yet, honey!

BLANCHE   How strange! I –

At the sound of BLANCHE'*s voice* MITCH'*s arm supporting his cards has sagged and his gaze is dissolved into space.* STANLEY *slaps him on the shoulder.*

STANLEY   Hey, Mitch, come to!

The sound of this new voice shocks BLANCHE. *She makes a shocked gesture, forming his name with her lips.* STELLA *nods and looks quickly away.* BLANCHE *stands quite still for some moments – the silverbacked mirror in her hand and a look of sorrowful perplexity as though all human experience shows on her face.* BLANCHE *finally speaks with sudden hysteria.*

BLANCHE   What's going on here?

She turns from STELLA *to* EUNICE *and back to* STELLA. *Her rising voice penetrates the concentration of the game.* MITCH *ducks his head lower but* STANLEY *shoves back his chair as if about to rise.* STEVE *places a restraining hand on his arm.*

BLANCHE   (*continuing*) What's happened here? I want an explanation of what's happened here.

STELLA   (*agonizingly*) Hush! Hush!

EUNICE   Hush! Hush! Honey.

STELLA   Please, Blanche.

BLANCHE   Why are you looking at me like that? Is something wrong with me?

EUNICE   You look wonderful, Blanche. Don't she look wonderful?

STELLA   Yes.

EUNICE   I understand you are going on a trip.

STELLA   Yes, Blanche *is*. She's going on vacation.

EUNICE   I'm green with envy.

BLANCHE   Help me, help me get dressed!

STELLA   (*handing her dress*) Is this what you –

BLANCHE   Yes, it will do! I'm anxious to get out of here – this place is a trap!

EUNICE   What a pretty blue jacket.

STELLA	It's lilac coloured.
BLANCHE	You're both mistaken. It's Della Robbia blue. The blue of the robe in the old Madonna pictures. Are these grapes washed?

She fingers the bunch of grapes which EUNICE *has brought in.*

EUNICE	Huh?
BLANCHE	Washed, I said. Are they washed?
EUNICE	They're from the French Market.
BLANCHE	That doesn't mean they've been washed. (*The cathedral bells chime.*) Those cathedral bells – they're the only clean thing in the Quarter. Well, I'm going now. I'm ready to go.
EUNICE	(*whispering*) She's going to walk out before they get here.
STELLA	Wait, Blanche.
BLANCHE	I don't want to pass in front of those men.
EUNICE	Then wait'll the game breaks up.
STELLA	Sit down and…

BLANCHE *turns weakly, hesitantly about. She lets them push her into a chair.*

BLANCHE	I can smell the sea air. The rest of my time I'm going to spend on the sea. And when I die, I'm going to die on the sea. You know what I shall die of? (*She plucks a grape.*) I shall die of eating an unwashed grape one day out on the ocean. I will die – with my hand in the hand of some nice-looking ship's doctor, a very young one with a small blond moustache and a big silver watch. "Poor lady," they'll say, "the quinine did her no good. That unwashed grape has transported her soul to heaven." (*The cathedral chimes are heard*.) And I'll be buried at

sea sewn up in a clean white sack and dropped overboard – at noon – in the blaze of summer – and into an ocean as blue as (*chimes again*) my first lover's eyes!

A DOCTOR *and* MATRON *have appeared around the corner of the building and climbed the steps to the porch. The gravity of their profession is exaggerated – the unmistakable aura of the state institution with its cynical detachment. The* DOCTOR *rings the doorbell. The murmur of the game is interrupted.*

EUNICE   (*whispering to* STELLA) That must be them.

STELLA *presses her fist to her lips.*

BLANCHE   (*rising slowly*) What is it?

EUNICE   (*affectedly casual*) Excuse me while I see who's at the door.

STELLA   Yes.

EUNICE *goes into the kitchen.*

BLANCHE   (*tensely*) I wonder if it's for me.

A whispered colloquy takes place at the door.

EUNICE   (*returning, brightly*) Someone is calling for Blanche.

BLANCHE   It *is* for me, then! (*She looks fearfully from one to the other and then to the portières. The "Varsouviana" faintly plays.*) Is it the gentleman I was expecting from Dallas?

EUNICE   I think it is, Blanche.

BLANCHE   I'm not quite ready.

STELLA   Ask him to wait outside.

BLANCHE   I…

EUNICE *goes back to the portières. Drums sound very softly.*

STELLA   Everything packed?

BLANCHE   My silver toilet articles are still out.

STELLA   Ah!

EUNICE   (*returning*) They're waiting in front of the house.

BLANCHE   They! Who's "they"?

EUNICE   There's a lady with him.

BLANCHE   I cannot imagine who this "lady" could be! How is she dressed?

EUNICE   Just – just a sort of a – plain-tailored outfit.

BLANCHE   Possibly she's – (*Her voice dies out nervously.*)

STELLA   Shall we go, Blanche?

BLANCHE   Must we go through that room?

STELLA   I will go with you.

BLANCHE   How do I look?

STELLA   Lovely.

EUNICE   (*echoing*) Lovely.

BLANCHE *moves fearfully to the portières.* EUNICE *draws them open for her.* BLANCHE *goes into the kitchen.*

BLANCHE   (*to the men*) Please don't get up. I'm only passing through.

She crosses quickly to outside door. STELLA *and* EUNICE *follow. The poker players stand awkwardly at the table – all except* MITCH, *who remains seated, looking at the table.* BLANCHE *steps out on a small porch at the side of the door. She stops short and catches her breath.*

DOCTOR   How do you do?

BLANCHE   You are not the gentleman I was expecting. (*She suddenly gasps and starts back up the steps. She stops* *by* STELLA, *who stands just outside the door, and speaks in a frightening whisper.*) That man isn't Shep Huntleigh.

The "Varsouviana" is playing distantly. STELLA *stares back at* BLANCHE. EUNICE *is holding* STELLA'*s arm. There is a moment of silence – no sound but that of* STANLEY *steadily shuffling the cards.* BLANCHE *catches her breath again and slips back into the flat. She enters the flat with a peculiar smile, her eyes wide and brilliant. As soon as her sister goes past her,* STELLA *closes her eyes and clenches her hands.* EUNICE *throws her arms comfortingly about her. Then she starts up to her flat.* BLANCHE *stops just inside the door.* MITCH *keeps staring down at his hands on the table, but the other men look at her curiously. At last she starts around the table towards the bedroom. As she does,* STANLEY *suddenly pushes back his chair and rises as if to block her way. The* MATRON *follows her into the flat.*

STANLEY   Did you forget something?

BLANCHE   (*shrilly*) Yes! Yes, I forgot something!

She rushes past him into the bedroom. Lurid reflections appear on the walls in odd, sinuous shapes. The "Varsouviana" is filtered into weird distortion, accompanied by the cries and noises of the jungle. BLANCHE *seizes the back of a chair as if to defend herself.*

STANLEY   Doc, you better go in.

DOCTOR   (*motioning to the* MATRON) Nurse, bring her out.

The MATRON *advances on one side.* STANLEY *on the other. Divested of all the softer properties of womanhood, the* MATRON *is a peculiarly sinister figure in her severe dress. Her voice is bold and toneless as a fire-bell.*

MATRON	Hello, Blanche.

The greeting is echoed and re-echoed by other mysterious voices behind the walls, as if reverberated through a canyon of rock.

STANLEY	She says that she forgot something.

The echo sounds in threatening whispers.

MATRON   That's all right.

STANLEY   What did you forget, Blanche?

BLANCHE   I – I –

MATRON   It don't matter. We can pick it up later.

STANLEY   Sure. We can send it along with the trunk.

BLANCHE   (*retreating in panic*) I don't know you – I don't know you. I want to be – left alone – please!

MATRON   Now, Blanche!

ECHOES   (*rising and falling*) Now, Blanche – now, Blanche – now, Blanche!

STANLEY   You left nothing here but spilt talcum and old empty perfume bottles – unless it's the paper lantern you want to take with you. You want the lantern?

He crosses to dressing-table and seizes the paper lantern, tearing it off the light bulb, and extends it towards her. She cries out as if the lantern was herself. The MATRON *steps boldly towards her. She screams and tries to break past the* MATRON. *All the men spring to their feet.* STELLA *runs out to the porch, with* EUNICE *following to comfort her, simultaneously with the confused voices of the men in the kitchen.* STELLA *rushes into* EUNICE'S *embrace on the porch.*

STELLA   Oh, my God, Eunice help me! Don't let them do that to her, don't let them hurt her! Oh, God, oh, please

God, don't hurt her! What are they doing to her? What are they doing? (*She tries to break from* EUNICE'S *arms.*)

EUNICE   No, honey, no, no, honey. Stay here. Don't go back in there. Stay with me and don't look.

STELLA   What have I done to my sister? Oh, God, what have I done to my sister?

EUNICE   You done the right thing, the only thing you could do. She couldn't stay here; there wasn't no other place for her to go.

While STELLA *and* EUNICE *are speaking on the porch the voices of the men in the kitchen overlap them.*

STANLEY   (*running in from the bedroom*) Hey! Hey! Doctor! Doctor, you better go in!

DOCTOR   Too bad, too bad. I always like to avoid it.

PABLO   This is a very bad thing.

STEVE   This is no way to do it. She should've been told.

PABLO   *Madre de Dios! Cosa mala, muy, muy mala!*

MITCH has started towards the bedroom. STANLEY *crosses to block him.*

MITCH   (*wildly*) You! You done this, all o' your God damn interfering with things you –

STANLEY   Quit the blubber! (*He pushes him aside.*)

MITCH   I'll kill you! (*He lunges and strikes at* STANLEY.)

STANLEY   Hold this bone-headed cry-baby!

STEVE   (*grasping* MITCH) Stop it, Mitch.

PABLO   Yeah, yeah, take it easy!

MITCH collapses at the table, sobbing. During the preceding scenes, the MATRON *catches hold of* BLANCHE'S *arm and prevents her flight.* BLANCHE *turns wildly and scratches at the* MATRON. *The heavy*

woman pinions her arms. BLANCHE *cries out
hoarsely and slips to her knees.*

MATRON These fingernails have to be trimmed. (*The* DOCTOR
comes into the room and she looks at him.) Jacket,
Doctor?

DOCTOR Not unless necessary.

*He takes of his hat and now becomes personalized.
The unhuman quality goes. His voice is gentle and
reassuring as he crosses to* BLANCHE *and crouches in
front of her. As he speaks her name, her terror
subsides a little. The lurid reflections from the walls,
the inhuman cries and noises die out and her own
hoarse crying is calmed.*

DOCTOR Miss DuBois.

*She turns her face to him and stares at him with
desperate pleading. He smiles; then he speaks to the*
MATRON.

DOCTOR It won't be necessary.

BLANCHE (*faintly*) Ask her to let go of me.

DOCTOR (*to the* MATRON) Let go.

The MATRON *releases her.* BLANCHE *extends her hands
towards the* DOCTOR. *He draws her up gently and
supports her with his arm and leads her through the
portières.*

BLANCHE (*holding tight to his arm*) Whoever you are – I
have always depended on the kindness of
strangers.

The poker players stand back as BLANCHE *and the*
DOCTOR *cross the kitchen to the front door. She
allows him to lead her as if she were blind. As they
go out on the porch,* STELLA *cries out her sister's
name from where she is crouched a few steps up on
the stairs.*

STELLA   Blanche! Blanche! Blanche!

BLANCHE walks on without turning, followed by the DOCTOR and the MATRON. They go around the corner of the building. EUNICE descends to STELLA and places the child in her arms. It is wrapped in a pale blue blanket. STELLA accepts the child, sobbingly EUNICE continues downstairs and enters the kitchen where the men except for STANLEY, are returning silently to their places about the table. STANLEY has gone out on the porch and stands at the foot of the steps looking at STELLA.

STANLEY   (*a bit uncertainly*) Stella?

She sobs with inhuman abandon. There is something luxurious in her complete surrender to crying now that her sister is gone.

(*voluptuously, soothingly*) Now, honey. Now, love. Now, now love. (*He kneels beside her and his fingers find the opening of her blouse.*) Now, now, love. Now, love...

The luxurious sobbing, the sensual murmur fade away under the swelling music of the "blue piano" and the muted trumpet.

STEVE   This game is seven-card stud.

CURTAIN

ACTIVITIES AND EXPLORATIONS

1 Keeping Track

A series of questions, scene by scene, intended to stimulate the beginnings of a response to the play. Used during the course of a first reading of the play, for writing or discussion, the questions will help you to keep track of character development, plot, themes and the writer's techniques. They should also be useful as a preparation for the more detailed coursework assignments suggested in **Explorations**. You could use the questions as a basis for a "journal" of your responses to the play.

Scene One

1 Look closely at the first long stage direction. How does Tennessee Williams use the sights, sounds and suggestions of smells to create a particular atmosphere? What atmosphere do you think he is trying to create?

2 The first visual impressions of Stanley, Stella and Blanche are important. What impression do you get of Stella and Stanley from their first brief appearance? Why is Blanche described as "incongruous"?

3 In a stage direction, the writer describes Blanche's manner as suggesting "a moth". What do you *associate* with a moth?

4 The place names used in the play have obviously been chosen carefully. Discuss, or note down, your associations with, or reactions to: Desire, Cemeteries, Elysian Fields and Belle Reve.

5 Why is Blanche visiting her sister?

6 What do you learn of Blanche's past?

7   How is Blanche received by Stanley? Do you feel a tension between them? If so, why do you think that tension is there?

8   Look at the last few lines of the scene. The sound of a cat screeching and polka music are used. Why?

9   What makes Blanche feel ill at the end of the scene?

Scene Two

1   Is there anything in this scene which suggests the childhood relationship between Blanche and Stella? Are either of them trying to recreate that relationship in the present?

2   Why does Stella try to advise (tell) Stanley how to behave towards Blanche?

3   What does Stanley suspect Blanche of? How do you react to his references to the law, and to "acquaintances" who can "appraise" Blanche's possessions?

4   Describe the contents of Blanche's trunk.

5   Who do you think "wins" the encounter between Blanche and Stanley? Give reasons for your answer.

6   Why do you think Stanley tells Blanche about the expected baby – when Stella had earlier asked him not to?

7   During this scene we learn more about Belle Reve. What are we told?

Scene Three

1   Tennessee Williams called an earlier version of this play, *The Poker Night*. Discuss, or note down, what you associate with the game of poker.

2   Why is Stanley on his "high horse" at the beginning of the scene?

3   How are Blanche and Stella received when they return?

4   Why do you think Stanley is annoyed when Mitch leaves the game?

5   Blanche says she thinks she might "bathe". You will notice that she bathes a good deal during the play. Why, do you think?

6   What impression does Blanche try to give Mitch about herself?

7   What do you learn of Mitch's background? Why do you think he is attracted to Blanche? Why is she attracted to him?

8   What is Stanley's reaction to the radio? Why do you think he reacts so strongly?

9   Does the contrast between the atmosphere in the bedroom and the atmosphere in the main room of the apartment strike you as particularly interesting? What are the differences?

10   How do the various characters react to Stanley's violence?

11   Describe how Stanley gets Stella to come back from the Hubbels' apartment.

12   Why does she return?

Scene Four

1   Stella tries to explain to Blanche the nature of her relationship with Stanley. Of his violence she says, "I was – sort of – thrilled by it." What do you think she means?

2   Can you identify in Stella's explanation any statements which seem to you to sum up how her relationship with Stanley works?

3   What is Blanche's plan for Stella's future?

4   Blanche contrasts the world of Belle Reve with Stella's present life style. Can you identify the main differences between the two worlds?

5   Stanley listens in on some of this conversation. Why do you
    think there is the sound of a locomotive in the distance as
    he first appears on the stage? Why do you think he does not
    immediately go into the room with Blanche and Stella?

6   Is Stella tempted to leave Stanley at any point during this
    scene?

7   When Stanley eventually does enter the room he embraces
    Stella and smiles at Blanche. What does that smile mean?

8   The scene ends with the sound of the "blue piano" – which
    is used regularly in the play. What do you think this
    particular music signifies?

Scene Five

1   It is possible to see Steve and Eunice Hubbel as an extreme
    version of Stella and Stanley (or some sort of indication of
    what Stanley and Stella might become). Do you think this
    view is justified? Is the fact that they own the building in
    which the two couples live of any significance? Contrast
    Eunice and Steve's way of life with the sort of life which
    Blanche and Stella lived in their past.

2   Do you think the star signs of Stanley and Blanche are
    appropriate? Why?

3   Why does Tennessee Williams have the sound of thunder
    heard in the distance at one point during this scene?

4   The stage directions in this scene emphasise Blanche's "fear"
    and "panic". What is she afraid of?

5   What does Blanche reveal about herself in the speech
    beginning, "I was never hard or self-sufficient enough"?

6   What does Blanche tell us, during this scene, about why she
    needs Mitch and how she will "catch" him?

7   Why does Blanche behave as she does towards the young
    man who appears at the door? Does what happens in any

way connect with what she was saying earlier? Does she see in this young man something that she has lost?

Scene Six

1 We are given the impression at the beginning of this scene that the evening has not worked all that well for Blanche or Mitch. Look closely at their conversation during the first part of the scene. Does the nature of that conversation help explain why their evening has not been a great success so far?

2 What do you learn about Mitch's mother and how he feels about her?

3 Blanche's story about Allan and Moon Lake Casino is possibly at the centre of this scene – and maybe at the centre of the whole play. (Scene Six is about halfway through the play). Why are these events important to Blanche? How have they shaped her life since?

4 Is this story part of Blanche's strategy to "catch" Mitch – or is it closer to her "real" self?

5 What do Mitch and Blanche have in common?

6 Look at the last line of the scene – "Sometimes – there's God – so quickly." Blanche is seeing (or feeling) a religious meaning in something. What do you think had induced this response?

Scene Seven

1 How would you describe Blanche's mood at the beginning of this scene? How would you explain this mood?

2 What does Stanley reveal about Blanche's past?

3 Stanley's revelations are punctuated by the sound of Blanche singing in the bathroom. Why does Tennessee Williams organise the scene in this way?

4   What do you think Stanley's motives are in telling Stella about Blanche's recent past?

5   How does Stella react to what she learns?

6   What do you think Tennessee Williams wants you to feel about Stanley during this scene? What does he want you to feel for Blanche?

Scene Eight

1   Does Mitch's absence contribute significantly to this scene? Why has he not turned up? What does his absence tell you about Stanley? Could you justify what Stanley has done? What do you learn about Mitch from his absence?

2   How does Blanche try to cope with Stanley? Does she succeed – as she did in Scene Two?

3   Why does Stanley bristle when Blanche uses the word "Polack"?

4   How cruel do you think Stanley is being? (Do you think he feels at all guilty about his behaviour – or proud of himself? Find evidence to justify your answer.)

5   What do you think the coming baby means to Stanley?

6   What part do the telephone calls play in the structure of the scene? (Why has Tennessee Williams put them into the scene?)

Scene Nine

1   Why has Mitch come to see Blanche?

2   Why is the polka tune so insistent during the first part of the scene?

3   Blanche says, at one point, "I don't want realism." Describe how she tries to maintain her illusions during the scene.

4   What does Blanche say she wanted from Mitch?

5 What do you think is the importance of the flower vendor's calls from the street? What is dead?

6 How have they "failed" each other?

Scene Ten

1 Why does Blanche break the mirror?

2 Why do you think Stanley undermines the reality of the Shep Huntleigh story and of Mitch's supposed apology?

3 Stanley talks of waving his pyjama top like a flag when he hears of the birth of the baby. Is his choice of "flag" significant?

4 What are his motives in raping Blanche? (Does the rape indicate sexual attraction or something more – something different?) Why does he say "We've had this date with each other from the beginning"?

5 The rape is accompanied by the music of the "blue piano". Why?

Scene Eleven

1 Do you think Stella knows about the rape? Is there any evidence in this scene to suggest an answer to this question?

2 How do you explain Blanche's retreat into madness?

3 What comment do you think Tennessee Williams is making in his organisation of the characters in the scene – the women with Blanche – the men playing cards?

4 How does Blanche's long speech about death draw together the main elements of her illusions?

5 How does the doctor manage to calm Blanche and lead her out?

6 How do you react to Blanche's last words before she leaves?

7 What do the last few moments of the play (after Blanche has gone) suggest to you about Stanley and Stella's future?

2 Explorations

1 Stories

(a) Tell the story of Blanche and Allan – how they met, ran away and what happened when they returned. Use Blanche's description at the end of Scene Six to help you, but add as much detail from your imagination as you can.

(b) Tell the story of Mitch and Blanche from Mitch's point of view. Include at least one scene in which Mitch talks to his mother about Blanche.

2 Scenes

(a) Write a scene in which Stella and Eunice discuss the events of Scene Ten in the play (the rape). How does Stella react to Blanche's allegations? How does she come to decide that Blanche must be committed to an institution? How does Eunice help her shape her decisions?

(b) Write a scene between Blanche and the doctor, some weeks after leaving her sister's apartment. How does she explain the events? Is she truthful – or does she convert the events into an illusion?

3 Reports

(a) Write a report from the high school superintendent (Mr Graves) to his school governors in which he assesses Blanche's character, her ability as a teacher and gives his reasons for dismissing her.

(b) Write the doctor's report on Blanche. What does he know about her past? How does he assess her condition? What does he think her long term future is?

(*Note*: Tennessee Williams says Blanche has a "neurasthenic personality" – see the glossary at the end of the play.)

4 Letters

(a) Write a letter from Stella to Blanche – some years after the end of the play. Is Blanche still in an institution? How is Stella's marriage? Have the events of the play had a long term effect on Stella and Stanley?

(b) Write a letter from Blanche to Shep Huntleigh shortly after the events of the play. How does she describe the recent past and her present condition? Is she asking him to "rescue" her from the institution?

5 Design brief

Put together a "design brief" for a production of the play. Outline your ideas on set design (with sketches), your advice on costume (with character notes) and your thoughts on use of sound. Justify your choices with evidence from the actual script.

A Characters

Blanche

HER PAST

(a) What do you learn of Blanche's early life from Stella's defence of her in Scene Seven?

(b) How did Blanche lose Belle Reve? What does Blanche say about the deaths in the family (in Scene One)? How important are these two experiences to her?

(c) The story of Blanche's relationship with Allan gradually unfolds during the course of the play – in Scene One,

Scene Two, Scene Six and Scene Nine. Outline the main events of their relationship and describe how these have shaped Blanche's life since Allan's death.

(d) How are Blanche's past actions, particularly in Laurel after the death of Allan, in conflict with the way she would like to be seen?

(e) Consider the following comment:

"*A Streetcar Named Desire* makes it clear that for Williams the act of fleeing always becomes the act of reliving the past. Flight forces the presence of the past on his characters as the presence of what they attempted to flee."
(Donald Pease in *Tennessee Williams: A Tribute*)

Do the "onstage" events of the play seem to you to be repeating any of the events in Blanche's past life?

HER ILLUSIONS

(a) What is Blanche's attitude towards alcohol? (Why does she drink? Why does she try to conceal her drinking?)

(b) Why do Blanche's clothes and jewellery mean so much to her?

(c) Why does she bathe so often?

(d) At one point in the play Blanche says, "I don't tell the truth. I tell what ought to be the truth," (Scene Nine). What does Blanche think, "ought to be the truth"?

(e) What does Shep Huntleigh mean to Blanche?

(f) Look at Blanche's long speech about death in Scene Eleven. Identify the main elements in the speech and show how they summarise Blanche's vision of what "ought to be the truth".

HER LONELINESS AND ISOLATION

(a) Does the way Blanche speaks in any way isolate her from those around her?

(b) Do her values (what she thinks is important in life) alienate her from the people she meets?

(c) What draws Blanche and Mitch together?

(d) What does she want from Mitch? Do you think the kind of relationship she hopes for is possible?

(e) Can you justify the view that Blanche's last words in the play ("I have always depended on the kindness of strangers") are a perfect expression of the sort of life she has led?

HER CONTRADICTIONS

(a) What does she think of the physical relationship between Stanley and Stella?

(b) How does she use her own sexuality – and to what purpose? (Look at her conversation with Stanley in Scene Two and the speech beginning, "I never was hard or self-sufficient enough…", in Scene Five.)

(c) Do your answers to (a) and (b) above reveal a contradiction in Blanche's approach to men?

(d) Now that you have read the whole play, how fitting do you think that early description of her being like a "moth" is?

(e) Do you think Stanley's rape of Blanche causes her final withdrawal into madness?

Stanley

(a) In an early stage direction Tennessee Williams describes Stanley as, "the gaudy seed-bearer". What do you think he means by this?

(b) Similarly, Stanley's star sign is Capricorn. What does this imply?

(c) Why do you think Stanley's actions are often accompanied by a blue piano/trumpet and drums, or the sound of a locomotive?

(d)   Describe Stanley's love for Stella. Does her patronise her? Is he tender? Is it a selfish love? Does he need her? When are they at their happiest? Does she have to suppress any of her natural qualities?

(e)   Do you think he feels threatened by Blanche's arrival? If so, how?

(f)   How important is the idea of "being master in his own house" to Stanley?

(g)   What do you think of his talk of the law and of worldly wise acquaintances?

(h)   Why does he go out of his way to be uncouth to Blanche?

(i)   How does he "use" the expected baby?

(j)   Can you see any similarity in the way he treats Stella and the way he treats Mitch?

(k)   How does his use of the English language contrast sharply with the way Blanche speaks?

(l)   Why is he sensitive about being called a "Polack"?

(m) Why does he challenge Blanche's illusions? Why does he rape her?

(n)   Do you think he feels any guilt after raping Blanche?

(o)   Do your sympathies for Stanley alter during the course of the play?

(p)   A recent critic said "Stanley is Williams's vision of the rapacity of the life force and the pragmatism of survival." Can you supply evidence to justify this statement?

Stella

(a)   Find evidence to support the view that Blanche tries to make Stella a child again.

(b)   How does Blanche try to undermine Stella's marriage? Does Stella ever go along with what Blanche says?

(c) In Scene Four Stella explains the nature of her relationship with Stanley. What does she say?

(d) What *price* does Stella have to pay for her continuing marriage to Stanley?

(e) Does Stella change during the course of the play?

Mitch

(a) What does Mitch represent to Blanche?

(b) Mitch is part of Stanley's world. What does he share with Stanley? How is he treated by Stanley? In what ways is he different?

(c) How important is Mitch's mother to him?

(d) What draws Mitch and Blanche together?

(e) How difficult does he find the early "courtship" of Blanche?

(f) Why does he reject Blanche? What does this say about his character?

(g) What do you think of his behaviour towards Blanche in Scene Nine?

(h) How do you think he will feel in the future about Blanche?

(i) How important is the inscription in Mitch's cigarette case? What does it tell you about the nature of his relationships?

B Themes

Presented here are a series of quotations, together with brief notes, which might be used as a starting point for exploring some of the themes which concern Tennessee Williams in *A Streetcar Named Desire*.

A useful approach could be to consider the quotations and notes, illustrate or support them with evidence from the play, and attempt some evaluation of the relative importance of the suggested themes in the play. Specific essay questions are included under **Critical essay titles**.

The themes proposed are by no means exhaustive, and it may well be that you will discover and explore what to you will appear more obvious, more important or more interesting approaches to what you perceive to be Tennessee Williams's central concerns.

1   The past

"Everyone carries around all the selves that they have ever been, intact, waiting to be reactivated in moments of pain, of fear, of danger. Everything is retrievable, every shock, every hurt. But perhaps it becomes a duty to abandon the stock of time that one carries within oneself, to discard it in favour of the present, so that one's embrace may be turned outwards to the world in which one has made one's home."
(From *Latecomers*, the novel by Anita Brookner, 1988)

"*A Streetcar Named Desire* makes it clear that for Williams the act of fleeing always becomes the act of reliving the past. Flight forces the presence of the past on his characters as the presence of what they attempt to flee."
(Donald Pease in *Tennessee Williams: A Tribute*)

Note: See the questions on Blanche's past in **Characters.**

2   Death

"Death is my best theme, don't you think? The pain of dying is what worries me, not the act. After all, nobody gets out of life alive."
(Tennessee Williams to a reporter in 1963).

Notes: Look again at what Blanche has to say about dying in Scenes One and Eleven.
Consider what Blanche loses when she loses Belle Reve and Allan. How important is the intervention of the flower vendor in Scene Nine?

How much do you read into the inscription in Mitch's cigarette case?
Is there a connection between dying and madness?

3 The South

(i) "I write out of love for the South... It is out of a regret for a South that no longer exists that I write of the forces that have destroyed it."
(Tennessee Williams, quoted by his mother in *Remember Me To Tom.*)

(ii) "... you knew you were passing through a ruined kingdom. The myths, even in the moment you discovered them, were worm eaten...The lawns and columned porticos were never far from the tangled swamps with odd flowers... And always drifting against the sky were the long grey-white tufts of Spanish moss on spreading live-oak trees. The live-oak was indeed a creepy symbol of the South, for in the sunlight and at a distance it was a majestic sight, and the Spanish moss trailed from its branches like the plumes of a jousting knight. As you get closer, the knight was slightly fly-blown. In the twilight the moss was a grey fuzz...and you saw that it was a parasite clinging to the outline of a healthy tree."
(Alistair Cooke in *Talk About America,* 1968)

(iii) "The Southern accent gives *Streetcar* its music, its irony, its lyrical plangency, its curiously decadent tone. These are not to be found on the page, silent. They are in that pervasive, strong, clinging accent which has so much of dispossession in it. Williams's plays are full of dispossessed people who we feel were once gentle but who find the jungle has caught up with their gracious clearings and spaces and the animals with their civilized pursuits. We hear in it, too, a kind of self-defeat, self-delusion, a weakness, so that we wonder what lies behind the gentleness, the civil behaviour."
(Gareth Lloyd Evans in *The Language of Modern Drama,* 1977)

Note: Some critics have noted that the battle between Blanche and Stanley is the conflict between the old world values of the South (see Blanche in Scene Ten, the speech beginning, "A cultivated woman...") and the aggressive materialism of the newer urban world.

4 Survival

(i) "The play, and its author, beg the question of the price of survival."

(ii) "His idea of heaven had turned into a hell of his own making."
(John Lahr, from an article on Tennessee Williams in *The Guardian*, 2.2.88.)

Note: Look at each of the characters and consider what they see as their salvation. Who "survives" the events of the play? Who fails to survive? What is the price of their survival?

C Critical essay titles

1   How concerned are each of the four characters with their own survival? Discuss their needs and how they go about fulfilling them, and evaluate their success in terms of surviving the events of the play.

2   Write a guide for two actors about to play Stanley and Blanche. Advise the actors on what you see as the two characters' main concerns. How do they behave towards each other and towards Stella and Mitch? Why do they behave in this way? Do they change as the play progresses? (It might help you to focus your ideas if you were to select two scenes and analyse them in detail.)

3   Discuss the importance of symbolism in *A Streetcar Named Desire*.

4   How are the past and the present intertwined in *A Streetcar Named Desire*?

5   "Williams has a very strong aural sense...a putting together of 'heard' and 'seen' materials." Illustrate this point (made by Gareth Lloyd Evans in *The Language of Modern Drama*) paying particular attention to Williams's use of set design, sound effects and the language used by the main characters.

6   Discuss the view that *A Streetcar Named Desire* is a play concerned with the conflict between the values of the old world and the new, and that this conflict is expressed through the battle between Stanley and Blanche.

7   Which character (or characters) do you think Tennessee Williams felt closest to in his play? Do what you perceive to be his feelings coincide with your own?

8   What do you believe Tennessee Williams is saying about human sexuality in *A Streetcar Named Desire*?

Glossary

Epigram This is from a poem by Hart Crane (1829–1932), an American poet who committed suicide. It provides a complex and interesting introduction to the major themes of the play.

Scene One

Elysian Fields in Greek mythology this was the place heroes went to after death.

L & N tracks a railway line for the Louisiana and Nashville Railroad.

white frame buildings of wood in the French colonial style.

"blue piano" black American blues music, used by Williams as a symbol for Stanley's primitive life force.

"Red hots!" Frankfurter sausages heavily spiced.

a Blue Moon cocktail a whiskey based cocktail.

a poor boy's sandwich bread, mutton and pickles.

a valise a small suitcase.

Desire/ Cemeteries place names in New Orleans – which really exist. A streetcar is a tramcar.

Por nada no trouble.

Belle Reve beautiful dream.

Poe Edgar Allan Poe (1809–49) writer of supernatural stories and poetry.

Woodland of Weir From Poe's poem, *Ulalume*.

high school superintendent the senior school administrator.

wire telegram

a feather bob a particular hairstyle – the hair cut in layers giving it a feathery lightness.

Polack	slang for Polish.
Jax	Jacksonville.
screen door	an outer door with mosquito-wire see-through panels.
gaudy seed-bearer	male, "macho", showy, crude.
Laurel	Blanche's home town in Mississippi.
not in my territory	a) not in the area where Stanley is a salesman; b) outside the world he recognises.

Scene Two

toilette	make-up, *etc.*
monkey doings	behaving in a silly way.
Galatoires	a French restaurant in the French quarter of New Orleans.
Napoleonic Code	after Napoleon III of France; the husband had ownership of the wife's possessions. Louisiana was formerly a French colony.
Lemon-coke	coca-cola and lemonade.
re-bop	trivial and evasive chatter.
epic fornications	large scale immorality.
tamale vendor	a person who sells hot and spicy Mexican food.
hot trumpet	evocative jazz played on a trumpet.

Scene Three

portières	an internal doorway covering, *eg* curtains.
one-eyed jacks	the jack of spades and the jack of hearts – seen in profile on a playing card, showing only one eye.
ante up	raise the stakes.
a sugar-tit	a baby's teat coated in sugar.
kibitz	to watch and advise a card player.
Xavier Cugat	a popular band leader of the time (late nineteen-forties America).

the "head"	lavatory.
quarters	twenty-five cent coins.
wrapper	dressing-gown.
Mrs Browning	English poet, Elizabeth Barrett Browning (1806–61).
Bourbon	a street in New Orleans known for jazz and striptease clubs.
bobby-soxers	adolescent girls.
Hawthorne	American writer, Nathaniel Hawthorne (1804–64).
Whitman	American poet, Walt Whitman (1819–82).
Wien, Wien, nur du allein	a Viennese waltz.
Potomac	a river.

Scene Four

wore his pin	a young man in the United States would give a "pin" to a girl as a token of his commitment to the relationship.
bromo	bromide – to calm nerves.

Scene Five

turn the trick	attract men.
fading	her looks are going; she is aging.
put out	be obviously enticing.
dime	a ten cent coin.
fifteen of seven	a quarter to seven.
Rosenkavalier	the hero of a popular opera by Richard Strauss.

Scene Six

neurasthenic personality	suffering from a nervous disability.
Lake Pontchartrain	an amusement park near New Orleans.

Mae West	a film star known for her "large" figure, her use of witty sexual innuendo.
owl car	an all night tramcar.
Pleiades	the star constellation "Seven Sisters".
Bohemian	unconventional lifestyle.
"Je suis la Dame aux Camellias! Vous etes – Armand!"	I am the Lady of Camellias. You are Armand. A well known romance in which a courtesan is "saved" by love but later dies of TB.
"Voulez-vous couchez avec moi ce soir? Vous ne comprenez pas? Ah, quel dommage!"	Would you like to go to bed with me this evening? Don't you understand? What a pity!
wash-coat	a jacket of light material.
Loew's State	a cinema.
Two-forty-first	an army unit.

Scene Seven

100 on the nose	exactly 100 degrees Fahrenheit.
no lily	not an innocent.
Barnum and Bailey	a circus.
ordinance	something like a court order.
Possess your soul in patience	A quotation from *Hamlet*.

Scene Eight

empty lot	Waste ground.
my beau	admirer/boyfriend.
cursed a blue streak	swear a lot.
Huey Long	Governor of Louisiana, assassinated in 1928, and remembered for his abuse of power.
get the coloured lights going	sexual passion.

Varsouviana	the polka tune which Blanche associates with Allan's death.
"El pan de mais" **etc.**	A Mexican folk song; the words mean "maize bread with no salt".

Scene Nine

robe	dressing-gown.
boxed out of your mind	very drunk.
"Flores para los muertos"	flowers for the dead.
"Corones para los muertos"	coronets for the dead.

Scene Ten

the glass cracks	seen as an omen of misfortune.
ATO	Auxiliary Territorial Officer.
Tiffany	expensive jewellers in New York.
put on the dog	dress up for a special occasion.
Mardi Gras outfit	a carnival costume.

Scene Eleven

Maldita sea tu suerto	curses on your luck.
Salerno	Second World War battle (in Italy).
Madre de Dios etc	Mother of God. This is a bad, bad, business.

Further Reading

File on Tennessee Williams	(Methuen, 1988)
Monsters in the Menagerie	John Lahr (*The Guardian,* 2.2.88)
Talk About America 1951–1968	Alistair Cooke (Penguin, 1981)
The Language of Modern Drama	Gareth Lloyd Evans (Dent, 1977)
Latecomers	Anita Brookner (Jonathan Cape, 1988)
A Streetcar Named Desire, with commentary and notes	Patricia Hern (Methuen, 1984)
A Streetcar Named Desire: a Study in Ambiguity	An essay by John Gassner in *Modern Drama* (OUP, 1965)
Remember Me to Tom	Edwina Dakin Williams and Lucy Freeman (Putnam's, New York, 1963)
Tennessee Williams: A Tribute	edited by J. Tharpe (University Press of Mississippi, 1977)
Twentieth Century Interpretations of Streetcar	edited by J. Y. Miller (Prentice-Hall, 1971)

Works which might be looked at alongside *A Streetcar Named Desire:*

The Glass Menagerie	Tennessee Williams (Heinemann Educational 1970)
All My Sons	Arthur Miller (Heinemann Educational 1971)
Miss Julie	August Strindberg (1988)
The Cherry Orchard	Anton Chekhov (1903)
The Widowing of Mrs Holroyd and The Daughter-in-Law	D. H. Lawrence (Heinemann Educational 1988)
Sons and Lovers	D. H. Lawrence